What these nonprofit board members are saying ...

"Dave Coleman is a focused student of nonprofit governance and now this book reflects his ability as a teacher. Any nonprofit board could improve 200% if they took seriously even half of these governance principles."

Robert C. Andringa,
Managing Partner, The Andringa Group,
co-author of *Good Governance for Nonprofits*

"A wise and experienced understanding of a wide range of nonprofits is evident in Dave Coleman's work. He now translates that into a highly practicable, usable, and readable book on board governance. I recommend it to you for reading and use!"

Steven G. W. Moore
Executive Director, M. J. Murdock Charitable Trust

"This is a very practical handbook for anyone connected to or serving on a not-for-profit board."

Jay A. Barber
President Emeritus of Warner Pacific College

"Dave Coleman accomplished just what he set out to do. Into a concise format that can be read in a few hours he has squeezed all the essential best practices of nonprofit boards. His writing is clear and engaging."

Jack Peterson
Consultant and Author of *Managing for Mission*, and Former President of Bellarmine Preparatory School

"Every paragraph breathes a gracious and penetrating wisdom, and makes obvious to me the commitment of this author to give you a thoroughly tested wisdom, trimmed of fat, and expressed with the economy and elegance of a true teacher."

Fr. Richard "Rick" H. Ganz, SJ
Vice President of Marylhurst University

"This book takes an informal but imminently practical look at important matters in the life of a board. Well-grounded, it offers valuable insights in a way that can be immediately applied by anyone serving on a nonprofit board."

Janis Bragan Balda
Professor of management at Fuller Seminary,
Instructor of nonprofit governance at UCLA
Extension, and a former Principal
at the Max De Pree Center for Leadership

"Dave's experience on the nonprofit frontlines, and as an analyst of organizations seeking funding have provided him a unique view into what makes for an effective and enjoyable board. He has condensed those years of learning into a very readable and well thought out primer."

Todd Silver
Co-president, The J.L. Darling Corporation

BOARD
ESSENTIALS

BOARD ESSENTIALS

12 Best Practices of Nonprofit Boards

DAVID L. COLEMAN

Andrew/Wallace Books

© 2014 by David L. Coleman. All rights reserved.

No part of this publication may be reproduced, stored in a retrieval system, or transmitted in any way by any means—electronic, mechanical, photocopy, recording, or otherwise—without the prior permission of the copyright holder, except as provided by USA copyright law.

ISBN: 978-0-57813-669-1

Library of Congress Cataloging-in-Publication Data has been applied for.

Andrew/Wallace Books is an imprint of BoardTrek Nonprofit Consulting (www.boardtrekconsulting.com).

CONTENTS

Introduction 1

Part 1: A Need for Best Practices
Chapter 1: There's a Reason 7
Chapter 2: Discovering 12 Best Practices 9

Part 2: Membership Best Practices
Chapter 3: Mission Focused 15
Chapter 4: Quality Membership 19

Part 3: Governance Best Practices
Chapter 5: Defining Governance 27
Chapter 6: Roles and Responsibilities 31

Part 4: Leadership Best Practices
Chapter 7: Only the CEO 39
Chapter 8: CEO and the Board Chair 43

Part 5: Decision Making Best Practices
Chapter 9: One Voice and Clear Policies 51
Chapter 10: Great Board Meetings 59
Chapter 11: Accomplishing the Mission 67
Chapter 12: Fiduciary Responsibilities 73

Part 6: Sustaining Best Practices
Chapter 13: Board Policy Manual 83
Chapter 14: Board Development Committee 89

Part 7: Acquiring Best Practices

Chapter 15: Taking Action 95
Chapter 16: Resources. 99

The Afterword Foreword. 103

Acknowledgments 105

Endnotes 107

About the Author 111

About BoardTrek Nonprofit Consulting 113

INTRODUCTION
"Begin With The End In Mind."
—*Stephen Covey*

ONE EVENING I sat in on a board meeting in which the topic of discussion was whether their organization's management should insert either a #5 or a #9 sized reply envelope in its monthly donor letter. Talk about micromanaging! I've also witnessed a board that simply could not make decisions, so negative circumstances made the decisions for them. I heard of one executive director who claimed he had his board on a "need to know basis" and he decided what they needed to know.

As a grantmaker, I have analyzed a number of organizations and found myself asking, "Where in the world was the board?" I've also found myself sitting in a boardroom looking at my watch as its hands barely moved, wondering whether or not I was wasting my time.

On the positive side, I've sat in amazement when effective boards worked well. I've been touched by the commitments of board members. I've seen the right people in the right room doing the right things. I've been blessed by board members who helped shape my life as an executive. I've seen boards think hard about what it means to take on a stewardship responsibility in their governing work. And I've left boardrooms energized about the future.

So why did you choose to pick this book up? Is it because you serve on a board of a nonprofit or because you are a CEO who has to report to a board? Are you new to the workings of boards? Have you had some negative experiences with boards along with the positive ones? Is it because you care passionately about your organization's mission and the way it changes lives? If you've answered yes to any of these questions, you probably have thoughts about your experiences, and likely some questions.

I wrote this book because I thought it might help you. I'm passionate about board governance. I've worked with boards all my adult life. I began by reporting to a board as a young executive director. These reporting relationships have continued through the years. But I also found myself serving on boards, consulting with nonprofits, and doing a good measure of writing about and training boards. Finally, as a professional grantmaker, I learned about the workings of hundreds of organizations and got a huge taste of what these nonprofits can produce, in part because of active and effective boards. So I've thought deeply about what good ones look like.

A couple of years ago I forced myself to think about what constitutes the basics of good board governance. I ended up expressing these essentials in what I call twelve best practices of nonprofit boards. I found that using them as a basis for board training helped members and CEOs identify specific action strategies for board engagement.

Then I wondered about communicating the twelve best practices to a larger audience. So I decided to write a short book, trying to get at the essence of good governance, hoping it would have wide readership. On my office bookshelves are a host of excellent books on nonprofit board governance, most of them considerably longer than the one you hold in your hands. All of them are filled with valuable information, concepts, principles, and answers. I hope you will pick up a few of them if you haven't already. But in the meantime, I fear that far too many CEOs and board members have not taken time to read them, or if they wanted to, they've wondered where to begin.

My goal here is to provide a handy volume that you could quickly read in one sitting, or by taking a few minutes each day to read it.

Who should read this book?

- CEOs (executive directors, presidents, etc.) who are committed to building a quality board
- New CEOs who are just learning the essentials of board governance
- Board chairs who want to be more effective in engaging their peers
- Board members who are committed to doing their best for their organization

- Boards needing a tool to use for in-service training on governance
- Newly elected board members who are getting oriented to their new responsibilities
- Consultants to nonprofits who want a good look at current best practices
- Students of good governance practices

You likely fall somewhere on this list and agree that a short read on board governance could provide either a good introduction or a helpful refresher for your engagement with boards.

When you read this book, you can expect to gain a better understanding of board governance. You'll also get a sense of how well your board measures up to a set of best practices. I believe you will find some new ideas, and perhaps a new commitment, to be more engaged in building a strong board for your nonprofit.

In the end, I believe you will find that a healthy board that knows the essentials and carries out best practices will impact your organization's ability to do even more to change lives. That should be personally energizing. And it should be deeply satisfying.

PART 1
A NEED FOR BEST PRACTICES

"Best Practice—best way to do something: the most effective or efficient method of achieving an objective or completing a task."
—*Encarta World English Dictionary*

Chapter 1

THERE'S A REASON

OUR PICTURE OF what boards do is formed by our experience with boards. It could be with a mature organization or a small all-volunteer outfit where the workers are the board and the board are the workers, or something in-between. Boards exist in many fashions—school boards, hospital boards, museum boards, church boards, and so on. They are all different in size, sophistication, agendas, and membership. Boards also function differently—some as a team of super-volunteers, others a group of cheerleaders, some as rubber stamps, a few as adversaries, and more often than not, the backbone of a nonprofit.

But for all of their differences, they all govern. Some just do it better than others. Maybe if we could get a big picture view of what really makes a great board, we would expect more from our own boards. And maybe if we expected more, we would do more to make them great.

There's a Reason

As a grantmaker for eight years, I had the privilege of looking at a couple thousand grant proposals, and personally working on well over two hundred. Besides reading about the proposed project for which funds were being requested, our analysis included a hard look at the organization. In the depths of the great recession that started in 2008, I began to hear colleagues in the philanthropic world refer to the organizations that had their ducks in a row as being the ones that would survive and emerge with a good measure of health. That made me wonder about the so-called ducks.

Nine "ducks" came to mind. And yes, if all of the ducks were in a row, my experience told me that a grant proposal would likely be stronger, and a grant would more likely be awarded. But often the ducks were out of line, and in some cases, almost missing. As a result, some nonprofits barely received grants. Others were denied altogether. But one thing was clear. There are reasons some organizations receive more grant money than others.

One reason is that as organizations, they have their ducks in a row. But getting your ducks in a row isn't just about funding. It's about excellence, about doing the mission, achieving results, and changing lives.

The Nine Ducks

About now, you may be asking, "Just what are the ducks?" I offer you my list with a simple command for each:

- **Mission:** Be passionate about your mission
- **Staff:** Build a powerful team
- **Program:** Create razor sharp programs
- **Marketing:** Market with a strong brand
- **Board:** Build an effective governing board
- **Office:** Let your office operation speak volumes about you
- **Funding:** Diversify strong funding streams
- **Financials:** Be sure your financial reports work for you
- **Planning:** Plan for tomorrow and beyond

Did you notice that the board duck was the one in the middle? It is because the board plays a role in every one of the other eight ducks. Boards guard the mission, hire the CEO, monitor program results, serve as ambassadors for the nonprofit, require good business practices, insist on sufficient funding, receive and act on financials, and approve the organization's strategic plans. Oh, and in all of that, they govern.

Yes, great organizations have good leaders. But they also have good boards, and on rare occasions, really great boards. There are reasons for good and great boards. They have the right members. They have board oriented CEOs. And they observe best practices. Of each of those organizations, it is often said, "They have a great board."

How is your board?

Chapter 2

DISCOVERING 12 BEST PRACTICES

THIS IS NOT a book about *the* twelve best practices of nonprofit boards. It is simply a book about best practices. In many respects a long list could be created. Dennis Pointer and James Orlikoff wrote a helpful book about sixty-four governance principles, ideas that are really best practices. My goal was to distill a larger body of content into a brief list that captured the essentials, and that people could get their brains around. As you read further you will see that each of the twelve on my list have multiple ramifications that could also be described as best practices. I am just asking that you stay with these twelve essentials, since I think they will provide a memorable outline for your commitment to building strength into your board.

I've divided the twelve practices into five parts as a way to make them easier to remember. Each one will be the topic of the next twelve chapters. I just thought you might like to see them all in one place before you get started. To help you to think about these best practices, I've provided some statements about boards. As they apply to your board, you can answer with a simple yes or no. If you are not sure, go with the answer that comes most quickly to your mind.

Membership

1. Boards are passionately mission focused
   - I believe our mission is important. Yes___ No___
   - Our programs align with our mission. Yes___ No___
   - I can explain our organization in two or three sentences. Yes___ No___

2. Boards are right-sized with quality members and relationships
   - Our board is just the right size for our organization. Yes___ No___
   - We are effectively recruiting new members. Yes___ No___
   - Our members take time to get to know each other. Yes___ No___

Governance

3. Boards understand and are effective at governance
   - I understand the meaning of governance. Yes___ No___
   - I understand the difference between management and governance. Yes___ No___
   - I am diligent about avoiding any real or perceived conflict of interest. Yes___ No___
4. Boards and their members are clear about their roles and responsibilities
   - Our board has its roles and its member responsibilities in writing. Yes___ No___
   - I understand the difference between governing and volunteering. Yes___ No___
   - I can explain our expectations to a prospective board member. Yes___ No___

Leadership

5. Boards supervise only the CEO
   - Our CEO is the only employee who is a direct report to our board. Yes___ No___
   - We have a good working relationship with our CEO. Yes___ No___
   - We conduct an annual performance review with our CEO. Yes___ No___
6. Boards have an effective CEO-board chair partnership
   - Our CEO demonstrates a commitment to building and having a strong board. Yes___ No___

- Our board chair does a fine job of leading our board. Yes___ No___
- Our board chair and CEO work well together as leaders. Yes___ No___

Decisions

7. Boards focus on policy, and thereby speak with one voice
   - Our board speaks with one voice, and members do not offer dissenting opinions after a decision has been made. Yes___ No___
   - We have open lively discussions and disagreements when wrestling with issues and making decisions. Yes___ No___
   - Our board has established written policies and has agreed to speak with one voice. Yes___ No___
8. Boards function with clear processes for meetings
   - Our board meetings are energizing, rather than draining. Yes___ No___
   - We have clear processes and protocols in our meetings. Yes___ No___
   - We don't need to make many improvements to our board meetings. Yes___ No___
9. Boards give attention to the future, end results, and big issues
   - We are clear about what we want our organization to accomplish. Yes___ No___
   - We have and are following a strategic plan. Yes___ No___
   - We are thoughtful and effective when making big decisions. Yes___ No___
10. Boards exercise fiduciary responsibilities for assets, income, and expenses
    - Our organization maintains sufficient unrestricted cash reserves. Yes___ No___
    - We have strong and diverse income streams. Yes___ No___
    - We are getting the financial reports we need, and are we using them to govern. Yes___ No___

Sustainability

11. Boards govern with a fluid and concise board policy manual
    - We could easily locate all of the policies our board has approved. Yes____ No____
    - We have a comprehensive board policy manual of 20 pages or so. Yes____ No____
    - We are attentive to matters that need to be expressed in written policies. Yes____ No____
12. Boards have an active year round board development committee
    - Our board has an active governance or board development committee. Yes____ No____
    - If so, I understand what they do. Yes____ No____
    - I know a person on our board that has an interest in helping us become better at what we do. Yes____ No____

Did you have a lot of yes answers? Did you have more no answers than you expected? Could your board be doing some new things to help strengthen its governance role and build a stronger, more effective organization?

PART 2
MEMBERSHIP BEST PRACTICES

"The most empowering condition of all is when the entire organization is aligned with its mission, and people's passions and purpose are in synch with each other."

—Bill George

Chapter 3

MISSION FOCUSED

Best Practice #1 – Boards are passionately mission focused

BOARDS ALL BEGIN with a mission. Yes, organizations have a founder, or a founding group. But they all begin with a mission, and they continue with a mission. Great boards, good boards, and even some quite mediocre boards have members who are passionate about the organization's purpose. Caring about something deeply is essential to an organization, its staff, and its board. I've watched men with a lot of years under their belt tear up when asked why they serve on a board. While I was making a visit at a Boys and Girls Club on a grantmaker site visit, a board member told me, "If you want to be on this board, you have to be willing to work, and you have to be passionate about kids." Yes, it is about the mission and how it changes lives. It is the mission that causes us to sacrifice our time and money, doing work that is necessary to make things happen.

My friend and colleague Robert Andringa writes, "Successful nonprofit organizations use their mission statements as touchstones for everything they do. They ask, 'Does the strategic plan and its supporting objectives build on the whole reason we exist? Does the budget accurately reflect what's really important to us? Do our policies and procedures advance our purposes?'"[1] If they do, we are mission focused.

Who Are We?

A good mission statement defines your organization. It articulates the fundamental purpose, is succinct (fewer than 30 words), and doesn't include content about strategies or programs. It also gets to the point, is memorable, and calls out the best in us. Boards often help write and always approve a mission statement. Mostly, however, they guard the mission, keeping programs aligned with the nonprofit's purposes, and avoiding programs that drift away from an organization's reason for existing. Mission statements answer the question, "Who are we?"

Future Scenarios, BHAGs, and Values

To focus on the mission and the future, sometimes staff members write a vision scenario; a multi-paragraph narrative that offers a picture of what the organization could look like ten years into the future. Boards are encouraged to get a feel for what the organization could be someday. A part of this scenario might include what Jim Collins calls the BHAG (big hairy audacious goal) that is one large measurable long-term goal that runs through a nonprofit's strategic plans, program development, and annual goals.

A nonprofit children's dental service may have as its BHAG, "A free dental clinic in all five low income areas of our county within ten years." Organizations may also list their values, identifying five or six important attitudes or beliefs that are ingrained in an organization's culture. These should be observable behaviors. Having just a few allows them to be memorable, and more likely, lived out. This makes it easier to make sure they influence planning, programs, and day-to-day activities.

The Elevator Speech

Finally, staff and board members often have an elevator speech. If you push the button that takes you to the seventh floor, and someone notices you are wearing a logo shirt from the organization you serve, they might ask about it. Your answer is your elevator speech—three or four sentences that grab the mission, what you do, and why it is important. For example, someone learns you are involved with Panhandle Harvest and asks about what it does. You respond, "We are a regional food distribution network whose mission is to see that no one in the Panhandle goes to bed at night hungry. We gather and distribute food to over fifty local pantries in our five-county region where the needs of individuals and families are met with groceries and a smile. I am a board member and love seeing the difference we make."

You say that with passion, in your own words, because boards are passionately mission focused.

> **Mission:** The purpose for which an organization exists.
>
> "The first task of the leader is to make sure that everybody sees the mission, hears it, lives it. If you lose sight of your mission, you begin to stumble and it shows very, very fast."
> —Peter Drucker[2]

Questions for Action

1. Do we have a concise and compelling mission statement?
2. Am I close enough to our programs to sense their heartbeat?
3. Do our board members have a basic elevator speech we can use to tell our story?

Chapter 4

QUALITY MEMBERSHIP

Best Practice #2 – Boards are right sized with quality members and relationships

ONE DAY, WHEN I was still new in my second executive director job, I had breakfast with one of the board members. "How is it that you joined the board," I asked.

He said he had an interest in the program and also had some friends on the board. They invited him to visit one of their breakfast meetings. After the meeting someone said, "See you next month." That was it. He was on the board.

Best practices call for a lot more intentionality than that, even though my friend turned out to be a good board member. First of all, board structure—which includes size, terms of office, meetings, officers, and committees—forms the necessary skeleton for a quality board. Members add muscle, skin, and movement. How members work together and relate to one another adds heart and soul, and can be a delight to watch and to participate in.

Structuring the Board

An often heard statement is, "We need more members on our board."
An often heard question is, "How large should our board be?"
All too often the answer to the first is, "Yes you do."
To the second, my answer is, and it is my answer only, seven to eleven members. I'm not comfortable with a board of five members. People get tired. When one member leaves, the board almost ceases to be a board. There are exceptions, but in most instances, a few more members help a lot.

On the other hand, there should be a good reason to have more than eleven members. However, if a board gets too large, it becomes more complex and there is a chance that its genuine effectiveness will be diminished. Writing for BoardSource, Charles Dambach says, "Experience teaches that smaller boards tend to be better able to govern. The smaller the board, the more important each individual member is to the organization."[3] I once met an organization that had fifty members, and heard of one with sixty-five members. Both appeared to have a working model. Yet for many organizations, seven to eleven members would be a step forward.

Members fill terms prescribed by the bylaws. Sometimes there are limits to the number of terms one can serve, like two terms of three years in length. Limits are a good way to give people an automatic out when it's time to leave. It also opens the doors to new people with fresh ideas and energy. On the other hand, you can lose good members. If a board does not have term limits, it needs to make sure there is an annual self-evaluation process, whereby members can disqualify themselves when they are no longer contributing to the board's work.

Board officers include the usual chair, vice-chair, secretary, and treasurer. Make sure they have defined roles, and functions. Sometimes a treasurer's role is to chair a finance committee, and offer a formal connection between the board and management in matters of money. Boards should have an audit and finance committee (sometimes the two are split) and a board development committee. There also may be other committees. Just make sure they can be justified and that they perform valuable governance functions. Sometimes a board can more effectively do its work with an ad hoc task force, carrying out a specific task during a short time frame and then disbanding. Having fewer committees generally keeps the board from getting caught up in matters of management, which is not a role of the board. When a larger committee structure is used, its governance function is to make recommendations to the full board, while it also carries out volunteer activities. These committees may be made up of board and non-board members, and could provide a place of service for potential new members.

For a local organization, board meetings could be held ten times a year. For organizations with a geographically distributed membership, quarterly meetings may be acceptable, with a couple of those in the form of conference calls. In any case, an annual board retreat offers not only an extended time to meet, but also a time for board education, attention to planning, and the building of relationships. Meetings should always be held in a private space, roomy enough, comfortable, and with refreshments nearby.

Board Recruitment

Remember that board members represent an organization's constituents, stakeholders, or those who are sometimes referred to as the "moral owners." Unlike a for-profit corporation, there are no other owners. Keeping this in mind, boards should be made up of people with different experiences, backgrounds, strengths, styles, and temperaments. Yet all should have a serious interest in your organization and its mission. Board members should often be reminded that we are all different in how we approach things, and as we appreciate this, great things can happen with a board. As new members are recruited to fill vacancies, it is helpful to keep this in mind.

All boards need a process for bringing on new members. There are numerous ideas on how this best works; recruiting, nominating, electing, getting a commitment, orienting, and engaging. It could take six steps, or maybe even a dozen. Rather than describe a process, here are seven principles for thoughtful board recruitment:

1. Get your organization's ducks in a row. The better the organization, the easier it will be to populate your board.
2. Know what board vacancies you have or will likely have. Meeting bylaw size requirements is essential, or perhaps, you need to adjust your bylaws to new realities.
3. Work on board recruitment year round.
4. Have a farm system—places for people to volunteer in your organization. Some will likely be identified as prospective board members.
5. Board recruitment is a task of both the CEO and the board.
6. A formal board recruitment process, in writing, and understood by all members, is a necessity, and needs to be followed.
7. A continued reminder that the board represents the moral owners of your mission is essential.

Board Orientation and Engagement

New members need to be formally oriented. An orientation meeting with board leaders, the CEO, and key staff members helps the process. A board notebook, chock-full of information, is a good resource that can be given to new members. An experienced board member can take on the role of mentor for the new person in order to offer help in learning the ropes and becoming more fully engaged. I'll never forget my entry into Rotary Club membership. Our club did a great job of getting me up to speed quickly, and tapping into the contribution I could make to the service club's motto, "Service above Self." If a board fails to orient and engage its new members, the likelihood of building a strong capable board decreases. Recruit, elect, orient, and engage.

Relationships

Not long ago I visited an organization's board meeting. Over a meal, board members had a lively conversation. Next, there was a time for members to quickly check in, sharing something that was going on in their lives. Then it was on to business and some serious decision-making.

Jay Barber, a friend of mine and former Warner Pacific College president and board chair at Mercy Corps once quoted a board member who said, "When I know the heart of fellow board members, I can better understand what is going on in their heads." I'm a big fan of boards that take time to build quality relationships among its members. I think one way of doing this is to have conversation over food, and then go on to the business. That's how I first experienced a great board, and I've found no reason to change my mind.

Board membership: Those who govern through participation on a board.

> "Many people seem to feel that a good board structure enables high performance. This is simply not so. What's crucial is the quality of our personal relationships."
>
> —Max De Pree[4]

Questions for Action

1. Does the size of our board match our bylaw requirements?
2. Do we have enough qualified and participative board members?
3. Does our board have a fair amount of diversity in experiences, contacts, outlook, and thinking?
4. Do we follow a written process of recruiting and bringing on new members?

PART 3
GOVERNANCE BEST PRACTICES

"Governance is the job of a board of directors."
—Susan Mogenson

Chapter 5

DEFINING GOVERNANCE

*Best Practice #3 – Boards understand
and are effective at governance*

THINKING IT WOULD be valuable, I recently took a graduate course on governance at Portland State University. It was definitely worth my time, but I kept wondering when someone would define governance. It never happened. On YouTube, Susan Mogenson defines governance as the job of a board of directors. When I saw that, I thought, wait a minute. You didn't define it! To her credit she did go on to explain governance. That's what my class did; the faculty explained it rather than defined it. That's what most of the books on boards do. They explain governance in a couple of paragraphs or a dozen chapters. I guess I wanted something short and simple. As one board member recently asked, "What's governance?" Like me, he simply wanted a definition.

Defining Governance

Here is my long definition: "Governance is the exercise of authoritative direction and control with the aim of guarding and nurturing an organization's fundamental purposes in a manner that is visionary, effective, efficient, legal, and ethical, on behalf of the public the organization serves."

That is a bit wordy and it includes some editorializing, so here is my short definition: "Governance is the authority exercised by a board on behalf of many to accomplish a mission with a degree of organizational excellence."

Essentially, the board represents the community (or whoever has enough interest in a nonprofit to be regarded as "moral owners") and serves as the organization's governing body. They define and guard the mission, and establish the results the nonprofit wants to achieve. They create policies, and hire a CEO who will lead the organization and the staff. This requires a determination of how authority will be delegated to the CEO, and how the CEO will be evaluated. Finally, the board establishes policies consistent with its own working philosophy, accountability, and the specifics of its role.

Governance differs from management. It is not the operation of programs, nor is it an extension of the organization's administration. Management is the responsibility of executive staff. Governance, a category by itself, is the unique work of the board. As for all of those other things associated with a board, like raising money, they are not matters of governance. Governance actually occurs in board meetings, between the raps of the gavel. Yet board members carry out other responsibilities, like helping to raise funds, but as individual members, and as volunteers. We will talk further about that in the next chapter.

The Duties

If you check with your state government about nonprofit organizations, you will likely find language to the effect that boards exercise fiduciary responsibilities. That is, they are entrusted to act on behalf of others in ways that exercise the duties of good faith, loyalty, and care. For example, they might say:

> Board members act in good faith and loyalty in a manner that one reasonably believes to be in the best interest of the organization. These duties require that board members maintain confidences, identify and disclose conflicts of interests, and never use information obtained as a board member for personal gain.

In the duty of care, it is often said that a board member must act as any *prudent person* would act in carrying out governing responsibilities:

> … one must make reasonable inquiries and exercise independent judgment using skills, caution, and diligence that a prudent person would use in handling corporate affairs.

In other words, there is real substance to the legal requirement that nonprofits have a board. If for this reason alone, good governance is important.

The Carver Model

You may have heard of the "Carver model" of board governance. Sometimes it is spoken of in a negative manner, though I think this is usually a result of not fully understanding it. Actually, the Carver model is "policy governance," a term that was trademarked by John Carver. When he was trying to make sense of what boards are supposed to do, he finally boiled it down to four things:

1. **Ends:** determination of what needs the organization wants to meet, for whom, and at what cost (a board role)
2. **Executive limitations:** determination of the boundaries within which the board and staff operate to establish methods and activities to reach the ends (a board and CEO role)
3. **Board-staff linkage:** determination of the authority delegated to the CEO and how that person's performance will be evaluated (board and CEO role)
4. **Board governance:** determination of the board's philosophy, accountability, and the specifics of its job (a board role)

Carver writes that the model "... is a job design for boards, a prescription for leadership by any governing board in order to enable the quality of leadership of which boards are capable." He goes on to describe it as "a complete operating system."[5]

In Carver's model, boards govern through the establishment of policies, through which they clarify what limitations they want to place on the CEO, and in turn, delegate everything else to the CEO and management for implementation. This clarity is designed to differentiate governance from management functions and to empower leaders. Compliance and progress are then monitored by the board. Personally, I think the model has a lot of merit, and I have been one of many who have adapted Carver's ideas for the betterment of board governance.

I include this brief and wholly inadequate description here because I will be referencing him several more times as we go on. Plus, you might want to jump to the chapter on resources where you will identify two of his books, a thick one and a thin one.

> **Governance:** The authority exercised by a board on behalf of many to accomplish a mission with a degree of organizational excellence.
>
> "*Governance* is an activity, an action word; it is what boards do. The essence of the verb *to govern* is being a steward and trustee of an organization's resources and capacities. Governance is a team sport. Boards exercise collective influence; their members have no individual power. Boards exist only when they meet, that is, 'between raps of the gavel.'"
> —Dennis Pointner and James Orlikoff[6]

Questions for Action

1. Would you describe your organization as having a genuine governing board, or is it more about supporting the leaders and the organization's operations?
2. Does your board understand the duties of good faith, loyalty, and care?
3. If you have heard of the "Carver model," what are your impressions?
4. Does your board have a formal conflict of interest policy, and do all your members sign an annual statement that provides any disclosure of potential conflicts of interest?

Chapter 6

ROLES AND RESPONSIBILITIES

Best Practice #4 – Boards and their members are clear about their roles and responsibilities

THE LAST TIME you joined a board, were you given a list of the roles of the board, an outline of membership responsibilities, and a set of expectations? If it wasn't in writing, was there a good explanation of what would be involved? I remember a friend telling me how she was invited to be on a board. "Come and join our board. It just takes a couple of hours a month." I've frankly stopped being surprised by how often board members are lightly recruited with little understanding of what will be expected of them. Perhaps that is why this best practice has to be highlighted.

Boards in the Real world

Real life boards have three functions. Newly formed organizations function with the mantra, "We've got it covered." Their role is operational. Without paid staff, members spend most of their time on the actual program, rather than governance. Their role is to make the organization function. As nonprofits grow and add a director and a few paid staff members, boards tend to shift their focus. Their mantra becomes, "We're behind you." They take on a supportive role, still do some volunteer work, and begin to get serious about governance. As more growth takes place, the board mantra becomes, "We're responsible." Governance rises to the top when actual governing practices are observed. Decision-making shifts from operational issues to strategic thinking and planning. Yet even seasoned boards continue to look to their members for support and operational involvement at some level. This is where board members need to begin to think about wearing two hats.

Two Hats

The governance hat is worn between the raps of the gavel, in deliberations and decision making. I like to think of this as my Mariner baseball hat. It's a big deal to make the drive into Seattle, pay the big ticket price, make the climb to my seat, and eat an overpriced hot dog. On the other hand, I also have a volunteer hat. That's my Rainiers hat, minor league baseball at Cheney Stadium a few miles from my house. It's less of an investment, and always a lot of fun.

In the nonprofit world, my volunteer hat takes me fundraising, assisting with programs, and maybe even taking on a chore for the CEO. My friend Steve sits on a board and does volunteer work for an organization that serves the homeless. He sometimes asks the CEO, "Am I working for you right now, or are you working for me?" He's figured out the two-hat scenario. When meeting with the board, he is governing. When helping with programs, he is volunteering.

Roles of the Board

It's time to put on your Mariner hat (or the hat of your favorite MLB team.) It's time to meet with the board, and do the work of governance. I've outlined eight roles for you to consider.

1. **Boards govern through mission-centered plans, policies, and decisions.** They govern, not manage. They approve plans that are more strategic than operational. They set policies. And they make important decisions, like hiring the CEO, approving the budget, or approving large unusual purchases.
2. **Boards select and work through the chief executive officer.** They carefully make this hire and establish a clear reporting relationship. They turn to their CEO to manage the organization by hiring other staff members and overseeing their work. Working through the CEO includes an annual review of his or her work, and making a decision about compensation. Effectively working with the CEO is at the heart of a board's governing role.

3. **Boards establish and guard the mission and the future.** Actually, for most of us, the mission was established earlier, and only on rare occasions do we get to be a part of writing a new one. Mostly we guard the mission. Instead, we make sure programs accomplish the current mission. We think about end results rather than the means to those ends. We are strategic and not operational. We make sure the organization is thinking about and planning for the future. We insist on goals. Yet we continue to honor the past. We care deeply about our nonprofit's ability to sustain itself over time. This is all part of our legacy as good board members.
4. **Boards monitor organizational performance.** Thus far we've been concerned about the question, "Where are we going?" Now we ask, "Are we getting there?" We begin with the goals, measurable metrics, expectations, and standards. Perhaps we create some type of dashboard, key indicators we can look at to know how we are doing. An educational institution looks at the numbers of prospective students, enrollment, retention rates, student scores, and the ratio between earned income through tuition and fees, and contributed revenue. For perspective, they compare the present with past numbers and current goals. Boards also monitor financial performance, fundraising, and management's compliance with policies that have been established for a number of issues including risk management and personnel.
5. **Boards take legal responsibility for the organization.** If you don't believe this, check with the IRS and your jurisdiction's office of secretary of state. Boards need to be sure the organization is in compliance with the many laws, licensing requirements, reporting obligations, and the like that relate to nonprofits. Some form of legal counsel is generally advised, along with policies about conflict of interest for its staff and its own membership.
6. **Boards carry financial oversight responsibilities.** Boards don't manage the organization's funds. They govern their management. They set financial policies, establish an annual

budget, and ensure that an independent CPA prepares the 990 IRS forms and an annual financial report. They also learn how to read financial reports, make sense of them, and act on them in a way that carries out fiduciary requirements.

7. **Boards commit to organizational funding.** It's not enough to see that money is managed, although that is necessary. Boards make sure there is a funding plan, one that is diversified, and is usually made up of a mix of earned and contributed revenue. For each of those categories, they also look for multiple funding streams. They insist on fundraising efforts by management. But a board's members also put on their volunteer hat, and participate in fundraising activities. In doing so, they are usually the pacesetters. Every board member will be a donor-of-record to the organization's annual fundraising drive.

8. **Boards maintain their own vitality.** They insist on capable leadership. They elect and orient new members. They see that the board gets various kinds of training. They insist on good processes, disciplining themselves in the practices of good governance. And they build relationships with each other as members, creating camaraderie as a board.

So Why Should I Serve on a Board?

I know you just had a lot of information dumped on you, and board work may not sound like that much fun. So please, catch your breath. All of those things weave their way into the fabric of board work, but you won't be doing everything all at once. Like riding a bike, once you get the hang of it, it's easy and can be quite fun. So take your time, keep learning, and it will all come together. Woody Allen once said, "Eighty percent of success is showing up." I think he was right.

Board Member Responsibilities

Showing up is where board membership begins. In fleshing out the role of the board, take a look at the responsibilities of board members. These are of two types, board governance, and organizational service.

Put another way, the Mariners hat or the Rainiers hat. The later requires the volunteer hat.

Board members have the following governance responsibilities:

- Faithfully attend board meetings
- Prepare for and participate in board meetings
- Take committee and task force assignments
- Participate in board development activities
- Observe the organization's work firsthand
- Support the CEO as a partner

Board members have the following organizational service responsibilities:

- Be an ambassador for the organization
- Be a donor of record each year
- Assist with fundraising activities
- Use individual skills and talents on behalf of the organization
- Use connections to move the organization forward
- Encourage and appreciate the staff, volunteers, and donors

When a board puts these responsibilities in writing, it often adds a qualitative or quantitative measurement. For example, instead of asking members to faithfully attend meetings, it creates an expectation like, "Attend at least seventy-five percent of board meetings." A board will do well to wrestle with and create specific expectations of itself and its members when it sets forth its own list of responsibilities. And when it does, it must place them in writing. Otherwise, they will have little meaning.

> **Roles and Responsibilities:** The necessary activities of boards and their members
>
> "The opportunity to be a member of a non-profit board is a special gift to us as persons seeking to serve and grow. It is also a special gift from us to society through the legion of organizations that are vehicles that make us a civilization. Seen in this light, membership on a governing board should never be taken lightly or accepted merely as an honor. It is a responsible and demanding job."
> —Max DePree[7]

Questions for Action

1. Does our board have its roles stated in writing?
2. Does our board have member responsibilities and expectations in writing?
3. Are these periodically reviewed?
4. Do our board members do a good job of carrying out board roles and member responsibilities?
5. Do we use this information in recruiting new board members?

PART 4
LEADERSHIP BEST PRACTICES

"Leadership is the wise use of power."
—Warren Bennis and Burt Nanus

Chapter 7

ONLY THE CEO

Best Practice #5 – Boards supervise only the CEO

A S A YOUNG protégé I observed an effective executive director. When I took his place, still at a young age, I had a board that took me under its wing, treated me with great respect, and mentored me. I will be eternally grateful to Stan and Paul, those first two chairpersons who contributed so much to my life as a leader. As a board, they were committed to their CEO. From the very beginning, I learned that I worked for the board and the staff worked for me. There was no confusion, even though I still had a lot to learn about supervising others.

I've concluded that there are ten things to know about the board-CEO relationship.

1. **The hiring of the CEO is job #1.** Don't blow this one. It is the most important decision a board ever makes. Use a carefully planned recruitment and hiring process. Take your time. Get the right person. Doing so could save a lot of grief.
2. **The board has just one employee.** While other staff members may give reports to the board, only the CEO actually has a formal reporting relationship with the board. This simplifies and strengthens the tasks of governing and managing.
3. **The CEO must have a written job description.** The CEO and board must agree to its contents. If one does not exist, I recommend that the CEO write one, and bring it to the board for discussion, fine-tuning it for eventual approval. When the job description is in writing, everyone will more likely be on the same page.

4. **Governing policies will provide boundaries within which the CEO works.** John Carver refers to these as formal executive limitations that become part of an organization's board policies. They say, "You have the freedom in how you get the job done, as long as you don't step outside of these boundaries." This provides a wonderful balance of freedom and constraint.
5. **Link the CEO's authority with the board's expectations.** Carver calls this the board-staff linkage. There needs to be an agreement on performance expectations, and the CEO must be given authority commensurate with his or her responsibilities. No one can be expected to be responsible without having the proper authority.
6. **Expectations should translate into a one-page annual work plan.** A set of agreed upon goals usually flows from a strategic plan, and becomes part of ongoing governance by the board and an annual performance review of the CEO. A work plan for the CEO creates necessary focus.
7. **An executive personal development plan is vital.** The board should see that personal and professional development of the CEO and staff is part of the organization's budget and the CEO's annual goals. Everyone needs to grow, and that takes a measure of commitment.
8. **There must be an annual performance review.** This is crucial to the board's role of supervising the CEO. There are many ways to go about this, and resources are plentiful. Just make sure there is an advanced understanding of expectations, a thoughtful evaluation process, and conclusions that are placed in writing. People like to know how they stand with their supervisor.
9. **Succession plans are a must.** This doesn't mean that your CEO is leaving any time soon. Yet departures do occur, and boards should have in their file some thoughts on who could take over what responsibilities, and what they need to know, just in case. The important thing is that the CEO and board have the discussion annually. It could well make a future transition much easier.

10. **Transitions are a reality.** When there is a changing of the guard, a carefully executed succession process can do a lot for an organization's health as well as the parties involved. Circumstances vary, and so must the board's response. In any event, the charge is to do it well.

CEO: The person designated by the board to lead an organization as its chief executive officer, and sometimes known as the executive director, president, principal, or administrator.

Four Questions a Board Needs to Ask the CEO in a Performance Review

1. How can we help?
2. Who is helping you?
3. What major problems are you having?
4. What are you learning?

"Executive Directors are the keepers of the vision in their organizations. They often lead the process to develop it, manage the process to communicate it in an inspirational way, and support others as they work to achieve it."
—Mim Carlson and Margaret Donohoe[8]

Questions for Action

1. Is the CEO the only direct report to your board?
2. Does your CEO have a written job description that is approved by the board?
3. Does your board provide a time for an annual performance review with the CEO?
4. When was the last time your CEO and board had a discussion about succession planning?

Chapter 8

CEO AND THE BOARD CHAIR

Best Practice #6 – Boards have an effective CEO-Board Chair partnership

---

HIGHLY EFFECTIVE BOARDS have excellent leadership. Robert Andringa writes, "Good nonprofits have good boards; and good boards have good chairs! The chair manages the board ... the CEO manages the organization."[9] Not only do these two leaders have different roles, their work complements each other. They work in partnership. Over the years I've had the privilege of working with some strong chairpersons who provided capable leadership of the board. I've also worked with some who were not strong leaders of the board, but who nonetheless were deeply committed to the organization. In every case, we worked in partnership. In every case, as a CEO, I drew strength from the relationship. This partnership is absolutely essential as a board best practice.

There are three components to this partnership. The role of the board chair must be clearly understood. The CEO must be board oriented. And these two leaders must work in partnership. For much of the material in this chapter, I am indebted to Robert Andringa, who has a long history of creating space for CEOs and board chairs to have meaningful dialogue and gain instruction about how they can be most effective together. In fact, some of the materials I have used can be found at his website, www.theandringagroup.com.

The Board Chair

The board chair can expect to spend about twice as many hours a month in this role as that of other members. An effective chair has a number of desired traits, including:

- Has good knowledge of the organization
- Possesses leadership qualities
- Is fair and objective
- Has the ability to delegate and motivate members
- Is an effective facilitator of meetings
- Is willing to make difficult decisions
- Is a positive communicator

As a result, great care should be taken in selecting the chair. Aim at naming the most gifted person for the role who is willing to do the job well. The selection process should be fair, perhaps involving a secret ballot during the annual board elections. Chairpersons often serve one or two terms, often two years in length. Because the role is so important, handing it off to a new person each year is not a best practice.

The chair's primary role is to ensure integrity of the board's processes, making sure bylaws and processes dictated by the board's own policies are followed. These will be discussed in a separate chapter. The chair leads and manages the board. The chair is the only board member authorized to speak for the board as a group. The chair should be a model board member. The chair helps recruit new members in conjunction with a board development committee. The chair makes or suggests committee assignments.

Of special importance is that the chair must ensure that the board behaves consistently with its own rules, that it deals only with those issues that belong to the board's decision-making responsibilities, and that any difficult board members are dealt with, quietly, in private, and appropriately.

The board chair has no authority to supervise or direct the CEO. That is the board's role. The chair is expected to advise and to partner with the CEO on all governance matters while being responsible for interpreting board feelings to the CEO.

The Board-Oriented CEO

I remember Robert Andringa dealing with this aspect of the partnership and saying he was convinced that no nonprofit board can move from good to great without a board-oriented CEO. Difficult or weak boards are often partly the result of CEO neglect. Board development is a vital part of any CEO's job description. Consider these eleven characteristics of a board-oriented CEO:

- **Legacy**: The CEO believes one of his or her lasting legacies will be a stronger board
- **Partnership**: The CEO sees a good board as a necessary partner rather than a competitor or impediment, and understands that the board's work is vital to the accomplishment of the mission
- **Role clarification**: The CEO helps the board clarify roles so that both the CEO and the board can move forward in their own non-competing roles, doing so with confidence and trust
- **Honors the chair's role**: The CEO honors the chair's role as manager of the board, and helps the chair fulfill that role without looking for credit for the resulting good leadership of the chair
- **Individual board members**: The CEO works with individual members, helping them identify their "volunteer hat," and encouraging them as board members
- **Performance review**: The CEO insists on a well-planned performance review, using an agreed upon process
- **Board updates**: The CEO gives the board excellent updates, in a format desired by the board, and as a result, there are no surprises
- **Committee assignments**: The CEO assigns key staff members to serve board committees
- **Administrative excellence**: The CEO sees that the board is well served, with announcements of meetings, the timely delivery of pre-meeting information, getting minutes out on time, making meeting arrangements, responding to requests by the board, and handling other details the board generally cannot do for itself
- **Board member recruitment**: The CEO helps, but does not dominate, in recruiting new board members
- **A board colleague**: The CEO behaves more like a board colleague by thinking, helping, and asking during a board meeting,

rather than as a "hired hand" only explaining or defending management

The CEO-Board Chair Partnership

These two people are the key leaders of a nonprofit organization. The chair leads and manages the board, while the CEO leads and manages the organization. In this way, their work complements each other. They partner with each other in establishing board agendas, committee assignments, ways to recognize board service, and improving meetings. I have seen many instances in which these two people meet weekly, or twice each month with phone calls in between. This practice allows for excellent communication and better leadership of both the board and the organization.

The CEO may or may not be an ex officio member of the board (by virtue of position.) In either case, the CEO does not have a vote since his or her role is to implement board policy. A good CEO has a voice that influences many votes by the board. While the board selects the chair, the CEO should be consulted about the nominees, and should have "almost veto authority" if he or she believes they could not work well together.

The chair often leads the annual performance review process, so effective communication throughout the year is essential. In board meetings, the chair must serve as disciplinarian with the board when necessary, rather than the CEO. The chair should also insist on some type of performance evaluation or input before re-election, and the CEO's views should be included.

Above all, the CEO and board chair should be respected colleagues, with each playing a critical role in the other's success as a leader.

Board chair: The elected leader of an organization's board

The Chair Must be Able to Perform Four Roles

1. **Ceremonial and representational:** Symbolizing and personifying both the organization and the board. The chair is often called on to be a spokesperson to both external constituents and internal audiences.
2. **Leadership:** The key aspect of which is influencing, motivating, organizing, focusing, and monitoring the board and the way it goes about its work.
3. **Facilitative:** Planning and conducting effective, efficient, and creative board meetings.
4. **Consultative:** Serving as a confidant and advisor to the CEO on organizational and governance issues and executive-board relationships.

—Dennis D. Pointner and James E. Orlikoff[10]

Questions for Action

1. Does your board chair facilitate the board meetings?
2. Is your board chair an effective leader of the board?
3. Is your CEO board-oriented?
4. Do your CEO and board chair appear to have an active and effective working relationship?

PART 5
DECISION MAKING BEST PRACTICES

"Plans go wrong for lack of advice; many counselors bring success."
—Proverbs 15:22

Chapter 9

ONE VOICE AND CLEAR POLICIES
Best Practice #7 – Boards focus on policy and thereby speak with one voice

A FEW YEARS ago I worked with an organization that unfortunately had a board of business people who simply could not make the hard decisions required of them. Coupled with an executive director who did not like to raise money, the nonprofit soon faltered and for a brief time closed its doors. Later resurrected by capable leadership, I am happy to report that they are doing well in achieving their mission. Good decision making is critical to the work of governance.

Over the years I've seen many good and bad decisions made, and unfortunately, have made some bad ones myself. As a result, I'd like to suggest eight principles for making good decisions. Good decisions ...

1. Support an organization's mission
2. Are consistent with the organization's values
3. Follow a solid understanding of the issues involved
4. Often engage a measure of outside guidance
5. Consider alternative choices
6. Make the best choice for the long-term good
7. Are made in a timely manner
8. Are supported by all members once the decision is made

This section focuses on the decision-making aspect of good board work. Effective decision making requires the board to speak with one voice, utilize written policies to express its intentions, have productive board meetings, set the organization's direction and know that it is getting there, and see that considerable care is taken in what is usually referred to as fiduciary responsibilities. This section of chapters deals with these matters.

The One-Voice Principle

Boards focus on policy, and thereby speak with one voice. In doing so, they place the specific directives of their decisions in writing, either in the minutes or as written policy statements. Then the board stands by those decisions. I remember one of my early board membership experiences. I was told, "Once we make a decision as a board, we all go from here in agreement. There are no dissenting opinions outside of this room." I winced a bit, because if I disagreed with a decision, I thought I should be able to say so later. I quickly learned I wasn't in Congress. If we acted on a matter, we had to act as a single governing unit. During the meeting, disagreement was encouraged in order to make good decisions. Our mantra was essentially "disagree and commit."

John Carver writes,

> ... the responsible board adheres to a very strict rule that the authority of the board resides in the board as a body, not in members of the board. If you are a nine-member board, you do not have one-ninth of the authority; you have none of it, while the board has all of it. We call this the one-voice principle, and not following it is a major reason for governance dysfunction. It requires the board, after sufficient debate, to reach a position that everyone may not have agreed with but that no one undermines. The one voice is not the chair's voice but whatever the board as a group, using whatever voting method it has established, has decided."[11]

The one-voice principle applies to all types of board decisions.

The Role of Policy

"Boards establish policies."

That is what people told me as a young nonprofit staff member. However, the only policies I could see that they established were the contents of a staff policy manual. Board members explained to me that policies are decisions and that they become part of the minutes. Then

I wondered how I would find those decisions without looking through pages of old minutes. Ultimately, I discovered that boards carry forth policies by memories, frequently being revealed by a board member asking in a meeting, "Didn't we decide something about that a few years ago?" So I spent a number of years with a murky understanding of how boards made policy.

Then John Carver came along, and I began to figure it out. Carver writes, "… the word 'policy' simply means written statements of what the board expects of itself or of those to whom it delegates."[12] I got that. But since a board governs rather than manages, and since it delegates to the staff all that it has authority over, how much policy does it need to write? Could it be that nothing should be left out?

Then I began to understand how Carver approached policies. The board spoke about its expectations (in some cases, delineating those things a CEO must not do in executive limitations) until it believed it could turn over the balance of authority for additional policies and procedures to the CEO and staff. Carver further states, "When you have as much authority as a board has, it is very important to have policies that not only control but also empower the other people in the organization who have work to do. This can be a difficult balance to find."[13]

In my later years of nonprofit leadership I served in a setting where there was an adaptation of governing with policies. I came to like what Carver called "executive limitations." Again, Carver writes, "Policy Governance boards set expectations about operational means by describing what would be unacceptable to the board even if effective … stating what is unacceptable does not draw the board into telling the CEO how the organization should be run, so the board does not need to know all the operational methods well enough to dictate them."[14] I discovered I could do anything I needed to do my job, except what the board told me I could not do.

For example, board policy stated that I could not overspend the operational budget by more than five percent. It also said I could not spend more than our current revenues. So for simplification, if the budget was $100,000, I could spend up to $105,000, if necessary. But there was another policy that stated I could not spend more than we took in. So here was a policy spending limitation. If we only had $95,000 in revenues, I was not allowed to spend more than that. As a result, I would have to make some spending cuts or raise more money to fulfill the board's expectations. The board delegated that decision to me, though I found it wise to seek counsel before making some decisions.

I thrived under that approach. While I felt more restraint from the board than I had ever felt, I also experienced greater freedom. The board had been clear about both the responsibilities and the authority it had delegated to me in the CEO role. At last I understood what it meant for a board to set policy. The marvelous thing was, the policies they established were less than twenty pages in length! How can that be? We will address that in chapter 13.

Hierarchy of Board Policies

To further clarify the role of policy, it is helpful to understand that there is a hierarchy of policies, with each being consistent with those above it, a downward flow of authority, and an upward flow of accountability. The following chart is helpful.

1. FEDERAL AND STATE LAWS A board expects staff to monitor on its behalf and comply.
2. PARENT/SISTER ORGANIZATION POLICIES Many nonprofits are accountable to another nonprofit.
3. ARTICLES OF INCORPORATION Seldom need amending unless name or purpose change.
4. BYLAWS Keep "Lean" and revise as necessary to reflect actual practice.
5. BOARD POLICIES MANUAL (BPM) The "one voice" of the board in an evolving, comprehensive document of 20 or so pages and a few attachments. • Mission, values, strategies, goals • Board structure and process • Board-staff relations • Parameters for executive action

Continued

6.	**CEO-LEVEL POLICIES** Planning documents, personnel manual, etc. approved by CEO and often given to board for information, not approval.
7.	**OTHER ORGANIZATIONAL POLICIES** Often determined in and by various staff units, for example: **Finance Fundraising Human Resources Programs**

(from Robert Andringa's Good Governance Toolbox; used by permission)

Two Kinds of Board Votes

Boards take two kinds of votes: decisions that are kept in the minutes, and policies that become part of a board policy manual. Another chart is helpful in bringing clarity to this.

BOARD DECISIONS (kept in minutes)	BOARD POLICIES (kept in Board Policies Manual)
• Proposed by CEO or board members • Determined by board vote • Kept in board minutes that should be filed safely for the life of the organization • Usually a short-term application of the decision	• Proposed by CEO or board members • Determined by board vote • Ideally kept in evolving Board Policy Manual (BPM) of approximately 20 pages • Could be ongoing for years

Continued

BOARD DECISIONS (kept in minutes)	BOARD POLICIES (kept in Board Policies Manual)
• Changed little, if any, when minutes approved at next meeting • Usually unrelated to Bylaws • Of limited use in orienting new board members • Little need to refer back to minutes after a year or so	• Changed as often as new data convince board it should be changed • Must never conflict with bylaws (or articles or government rules) • An essential document for orienting new board members • Important to review/update BPM at every meeting
Examples of Board Decisions	Examples of Board Policies
• Approve an agenda • Approve a financial report • Approve previous minutes • Appoint or terminate a CEO • Elect a board member or officer • Adopt a budget • Approve a new program • Pass resolution of commendation • Etc.	• Mission, values, strategies • Majors goals • Committees and their make-up • Criteria for new board members • Evaluation process for CEO • Guidelines for finances • Limitations on program activities • Parameters around fundraising • Etc.

(from Robert Andringa's Good Governance Toolbox; used by permission)

Once a board has a clear understanding of how decisions are made, how policies work, and the one-voice principle, it is on its way to greater effectiveness. These will play out within the processes used in board meetings.

> **Policy**: Written statements by the board of its expectations of itself, its CEO, and the organization.
>
> "Deliberate in many voices, but govern as one."
> —John Carver [15]

Questions for Action

1. Does our board speak with one voice after decisions are made?
2. Do we understand what it means to make policy?
3. Can we easily access all of the policies our board has established in one place?
4. Have we differentiated between board-established policies and those created by management for day-to-day operations?

Chapter 10

GREAT BOARD MEETINGS

Best Practice #8 – Boards function with clear processes for meetings

THE BOARD MEETING is the centerpiece of board governance. It is here that members assemble and go about governing. It is here that decisions are made, and as a result, the staff receives its marching orders to lead and manage the organization. As a result, thoughtfulness should go into the preparation of every board meeting. Board processes need to be followed. Members should come prepared. And the chair should effectively facilitate the interactions and decision making. Good governance takes place in this setting.

As an outsider, I remember watching one board carry out its work in a most effective manner, everyone playing his or her part, being highly engaged, and being very productive. It was like watching a sports team play at the peak of its game. More often than not, these are the kinds of meetings in which members are energized, and walk away with the conviction that serving on the board is well worth their time.

Governing Style as Policy

Governing style is another way of talking about board processes. It is helpful if a board states this as a policy regarding its own practices, reviews it from time to time, and uses it as a guide for how the board functions. What follows is an example of how one board decided to define its processes:

Governing Style. The board will approach its task with a style that emphasizes policy, outward vision, encouragement of diversity in viewpoints, and strategic leadership more than administrative detail, clear distinctions between board and staff roles, and pro-activity rather than re-activity. In this spirit the board will:

1. Enforce upon itself and its members whatever discipline is needed to govern with excellence. Discipline will apply to matters such as attendance, respect of clarified roles, speaking with one voice, and self-policing of any tendency to stray from governance adopted in these board policies.
2. Be accountable to the public for competent, conscientious and effective accomplishment of its obligations as a body. It will allow no officer, individual or committee of the board to usurp this role or hinder its commitment.
3. Monitor and regularly discuss the board's own process and performance, seeking to ensure the continuity of its governance capability by selection, orientation, training, and evaluation of board members.
4. Be responsible for its own performance, but seek to encourage assistance from the CEO in the board's pursuit of excellence.

Protocol: Rules of the Road

Boards have generally understood and unwritten ways they do things—protocols, or rules of the road for conducting their meetings. It is often a good idea to have these in writing as reminders of how people will work together in a group process to carry out its work. I was in a boardroom of one organization and noted the following list that appeared to apply to both board and staff meetings.

1. Meetings will start on time
2. Meetings will end five minutes prior to the published time
3. Silence will be interpreted as consent
4. Agenda items as defined on the agenda will be followed
5. Decisions will be determined by a majority vote
6. Attendees will own and support all decisions
7. Attendees will respect and accept all reminders to remain focused

They were serious about how they went about their work. If a list of protocols were drawn up that described how your board operates, what would it look like?

Time and Place

Establish an annual calendar of board meetings and key events for your organization. Once established, and members have all meetings on their own calendars, stick to your plan. Remember too that good meetings have a published starting and ending time and adherence will be appreciated by all members and those waiting for them at home. Meetings should be held in a comfortable and private setting, with appropriate AV equipment, beverages, and snacks. For boards with out-of-town members, arrangements need to be made for transportation and lodging.

Creating the Agenda

How are the agendas for your board meetings created? Hopefully, they are the collaborative work of the board chair and CEO, building an agenda that best reflects board processes, input from board members, and the needs at hand. The agenda should be prepared at least a week in advance and distributed to members. A good agenda will include a scheduled time for each item in order to keep things moving forward so the meeting will end on time. Some organizations find a consent agenda to be a helpful tool. It is simply a list of agenda items that need to be approved as a formality, and that are often preceded by board members having read the appropriate information prior to the meeting. The consent agenda and its list of items appear as part of the overall agenda. Since no discussion is required, only a vote is needed.

Richard Chait and his colleagues suggest that boards typically engage in two types of governance activity. They call the first type *fiduciary*. Members are concerned about the stewardship of tangible assets, so everyone looks down at the reports before them and does a measure of hard thinking. The second type is *strategic*. Members are engaged with management in the broad strokes of the organization's mission and future. In this type of governance activity, members look outward, and often dream about things to come. However, Chait and his colleagues argue for a third type, which they call *generative* thinking. Members in this mode sit around the boardroom table pondering the large leadership issues of an organization as it operates in an ever-changing world. Chait believes that too often this type of work does not get done by boards, which is unfortunate, because it offers productive and energizing leadership.[16] Board leaders may want to learn more about this type of thinking, and include a blend of all three activities in their deliberations. And for faith-based organizations, boards using the generative mode may find themselves wrestling with the integration of their deeply held beliefs and the work of governance.

Attached to the agenda should be other documents for members to study in advance of the meeting, including minutes from the previous meeting, a CEO report, current financials, appropriate program updates, and background information on any proposals that require a decision, including the wording of proposed policy changes.

For mid-sized and large organizations, it is a good practice to utilize an internal website, or even a professional web service designed to manage board information. It is wise to send an e-mail reminder regarding board meetings a few days in advance, and a reminder that if unable to attend, the office should be notified.

Meeting Content

As a young staff member, I attended our organization's board meetings which were held in a room at a restaurant. I enjoyed a steak, fully loaded baked potato, salad, and at the end, a piece of strawberry pie. Conversation around the table was informal, as it became evident to me that relationships were important to this group. Once dinner was over, the business began. From those early days I became convinced of the importance of building relationships among board members, and having a conversation over a meal is a good way for that to happen. These informal times also set the stage for productive board work.

The agenda should begin with lighter content, move to heavier business items, and end on the lighter side. Some educational time, both related to board governance and your organization's work can be included as a way to be better at what you do. Using a "minute for mission" might help everyone learn more about the organization's programs and results. One idea is to have board members do some of these reports after they have engaged with staff and program participants on the frontlines of the organization's work. Committee reports should focus on board activity, rather than management issues. Meetings should in some way also address these two vital questions: "Where are we going?" and "How are we doing in getting there?" If the board needs time for everyone to put on his or her volunteer hat, say doing some work on an organization's next fundraising gala, this could be done following the formal agenda of the board meeting.

Meeting Facilitation and Deliberations

At the heart of a good board is the facilitation of the meeting and its deliberations. Here are some thoughts:

- Usually the board chair facilitates, though sometimes the CEO or a committee chair may be asked to facilitate some portion of the meeting
- For some issues, have complex resolutions drafted, reviewed, and distributed in advance
- Set time limits for discussion and avoid being derailed by minor issues
- On major issues, consider a pre-meeting several days in advance so members can become more informed about the issue at hand
- For large boards, use quickly formed small groups to get more dialogue
- Gain consensus during discussion to be sure all points of view have been aired
- The chair or facilitator should continue to clarify and be sure all members have been heard
- The chair should summarize follow-up action items

Follow-up

Let me offer two suggestions.

- **Board chair's follow-up message:** It should be the responsibility of the board chair to identify any action items all board members have agreed to, and any specific actions agreed to by individual board members. Once this is done, these assignments should be sent out electronically by the board chair on the day following

the board meeting. The message should come with a "Print This" headline, so members can use the list as a reminder of what they have committed to do between now and the next board meeting.
- **Office communication:** Within a week the office should send minutes to members along with, if applicable, an updated board policies manual. In some cases, members will simply be notified that these items have been posted on the organization's internal website.

Ten Suggestions for Board Members

When thinking about how you will better serve your board, let me offer ten suggestions I have found helpful.

1. Mark board meeting times on your calendar for a full year, and avoid unnecessary conflicts
2. Make attendance a priority; if for some reason you cannot attend, call the chair or office
3. Arrive on time and stay until the end
4. Participate, knowing that on some issues you will bring extra insights to the discussion and decision making
5. Prepare, having completed any assignment you or your committee was assigned or volunteered for
6. Don't be afraid to ask inquiring and even difficult questions that relate to the discussion at hand
7. Don't waste time on mundane day-to-day management issues or matters that require staff action rather than board decisions; sometimes you may want to discuss a matter with the CEO outside of the regular meeting
8. Keep your eye on the mission and the organization's plans and goals
9. Do your part to create an emotionally safe environment where everyone feels free to express his or her views, cheerfully serving in a climate of mutual respect
10. At the end of the meeting, be sure your personal follow-up steps are clearly understood

Board Retreats

From my experience, an annual board retreat is a must. Again and again as I met with organizations about a proposed grant, I heard from boards about their effective utilization of an annual retreat. I've also had the privilege of facilitating a number of retreats, and have come to believe in their value. Retreats help build relationships, create opportunities for team building, and usually accomplish some specific emphasis (education, board training, annual planning, strategic planning, etc.) I think the best option is an overnight retreat. But I have also seen one-day or even a half-day retreat achieve good results. Consider utilizing an outside speaker and/or an outside professional facilitator.

> **Processes:** The manner in which a board chooses to govern when it meets.
>
> "There is simply no substitute for a good meeting—a dynamic, passionate, and focused engagement—when it comes to extracting the collective wisdom of a team."
>
> —Patrick Lencioni[17]

Questions for Action

1. Do we get a well-planned agenda and background information comfortably in advance of the board meeting?
2. Do we have clearly stated governing processes and protocols or rules of the road about how we conduct our business?
3. Do we have a one-year calendar of board meetings and key organizational events involving the board?
4. Are our board meetings energizing or draining?

Chapter 11

ACCOMPLISHING THE MISSION

*Best Practice # 9 – Boards give attention to
the future, end results, and big issues*

OUR FIRST BEST practice, that boards are passionately mission-focused, returns us to the details of what it means to see that the mission is effectively carried out. The central role of a governing board is to establish and guard the mission and the future. Sometimes a board is called on to restate the mission. But for the most part, boards help keep the organization focused and avoid mission drift. I've primarily worked for two organizations over the years, one that was founded in 1944, and one in 1974. In both cases, there has been virtually no mission drift over their long histories. Their purposes remain intact. The same values have continued to drive them over the years. In both cases, their boards are to be commended for their leadership.

As a result, boards deal with two fundamental questions, focus on end results, and make sure plans are in place to accomplish the mission.

The Mission and End Results

I've placed considerable emphasis on the mission of your nonprofit, as have many writers. The role of your organization is to achieve its stated purposes, and to do so on behalf of those who have a vested interest in what you do. John Carver speaks less about the mission, and states that organizations are about *ends* and *means*—what you desire as a result, and how you get there. He regards boards as more interested in the ends, while management digs into the details of the means to achieving those ends. In governance, the means are generally guided by established board polices. In terms of what he calls *ends*, using the words of this author, Carver raises three questions that must be asked:

1. What specifically are we seeking to accomplish in living out our mission?
2. Who are the intended recipients of our efforts?
3. What will it cost (including the choice to eliminate less important programs)[18]

How much discussion has your board had regarding these questions? Answering them is critical to your success.

Two Questions

As a result, your board must always be asking two other fundamental questions:

1. Where are we going?
2. How are we doing in getting there?

One sets the direction while the other monitors the progress. In between those two questions rests the day-to-day operation of your nonprofit and its programs. Unfortunately, that is where too many boards spend most of their time rather than focusing on the larger picture. After all, programs need to be funded, money must be stewarded, risks need to be managed, staff must be hired, and programs need to be created. Yet those two big questions belong in every meeting, and they flow from the above penetrating questions asked by Carver.

Enter the Strategic Plan

There is much written about strategic planning, and there are people to help guide your organization through a strategic planning process. So I will not go into much detail. I do believe, however, that before any planning begins, organizations need to think through what they want out of strategic planning, and prepare accordingly. For example, I believe strategic thinking is at the forefront of planning. What essential realities, internal and external, must be addressed? Is there any significant trend or factor that will impact the organization's future—what my friend and colleague Jim Galvin calls the "kernel"? This may be the key ingredient in effective planning. Generative discussions, as Chait calls them, occur at this point. From there, I like a five-year plan, but one that is revisited in a strategic planning process every three years. Five years offers a longer look, but three years takes into account the changes that take place in our organizations and their external environments. So in my opinion, at three-year intervals, a new five-year plan is in order.

I would like to suggest that good strategic planning involves looking at the organization from four vista points. Typically planners look at going *deeper*. That is, they think about expanding current programs in the same location. But they also explore the idea of going *wider*. New programs and new locations may be added to expand the nonprofit's reach. As important as these are, there are, I believe, two other vistas that are foundational. Being *stronger* means that capacity needs to be strengthened. Administrative staffing, cash reserves, funding development efforts, and information technology all come to mind. Finally and often ignored, is being *wiser*. Again, here is the "kernel." Assumptions are challenged, current realities in the organization's external environment are scanned, large questions are asked, and deep thinking is done.

I also like the metaphors of the journey and the role of the guide. As a result, I like to think of the strategic plan as the roadmap to the future. Your mission and end results are the destination. But you must determine how you will get there, and that may require finding someone to help guide the process such as a professional facilitator.

Should the board do the strategic planning, or should the staff? Who needs to approve a final strategic plan? Every organization needs to answer these questions in a way that best fits its needs. Frankly, I like to see the board involved, though for large organizations, their attention should be on the largest issues. I also believe the board needs to approve the plan, though some would disagree and would leave the strategic plan up to management. As I said, strategic planning itself needs to be planned, with the board agreeing on the overall strategy for its use.

Business Plans and Budgets

Strategic plans ultimately lead to business plans, cash flow estimates, growth projections, and the like. Without this level of planning, usually done by management, strategic plans can turn into pie in the sky. It is vital that this type of planning receives a high degree of research and realism, placed alongside of the dreaming that goes into future directions. High caliber board members often want to see these plans or pro forma, and hear about how the projections were made. Good governance asks those kinds of big and important questions.

The Powerful Role of the Annual Plan

Awhile back, I facilitated a board retreat for an organization. After completing the creation of their three-year strategic plan a year earlier, they established an annual plan with a clear set of objectives. At the retreat, they reviewed the past year, and set forth the basics for the annual plan for year two. In other words, the board knew where the organization was going, how it was doing in getting there, and what the next steps should be.

This is the power of an annual plan. May I suggest that it be summarized into five to ten measurable goals. Some of the goals will be metric based, while others will be answered based on whether a specific action was taken or not. This summary, with up-to-date answers to the "How are we doing" question, should be part of every board meeting. In effect, you are following the road map, and you know exactly where you are on the journey.

Measuring Results

The old management adage is that what gets measured gets done. That is why goals are important. Getting results for some objectives will be clear. For example, "We have 400 members, and our goal next year is to have 500." Yet that measures only an input that leads to accomplishing the actual mission. It will be more difficult to measure the results of what happens to those members. Peter Drucker reminds us that nonprofits are about changing lives.[19] That is often hard to measure. Yet increasingly, there are ways to get at some understanding of what is happening in people's lives, and whether or not an organization is making a difference. Yes, there is activity. But is it actually accomplishing the mission?

Dashboards

A recent trend is for boards to create a basic dashboard of information they want to monitor, seeing current results in relationship to past performance and future projections. While management may be measuring many items, a board needs to focus on critical information related to its role of governance. What information should your organization watch in terms of programs, both in terms of quality and quantity? A regional food bank may look at pounds of food, dollar value of food, number of food pantries served, and the number of visitors to those pantries. Nonprofits also need to watch their financial information, a subject that will be addressed in the next chapter. Perhaps it is time for your board to create a basic dashboard with information it should have to more successfully govern. Once this is done, deciding on how it is presented visually will help make it more effective in keeping the board informed.

Reporting Results

Because your organization has responsibilities to the public, I believe that some form of public annual report is in order. In grantmaking, I've seen dozens and dozens of them. Some are quite sophisticated, creative, and expensive. Others are rather simple, obviously done on a limited budget. An increasing number now appear on organization websites, with a simple notification to donors that it is available. All communicate a nonprofit's results, progress, major events, and finances. All communicate a measure of transparency to the public. All answer the two questions about where the organization is going and whether or not it is getting there.

Attention: Those concerns a board cares about most and upon which it offers its primary focus.

"If Peter Drucker were with you and your organization today, we believe he would ask the same questions of you that he asked more than fifteen years ago: What is our mission? Who is our customer? What does the customer value? What are our results? What is our plan?"

—Frances Hesselbein
(in the foreword to Drucker's book)[20]

Questions for Action

1. Do we know what the end results of our programs should be? And can they be measured?
2. Do our programs align with our stated mission?
3. Do we have an up-to-date strategic plan?
4. Does our organization have an annual set of goals that is shared by the board and management?
5. Do we keep our public well informed?

Chapter 12

FIDUCIARY RESPONSIBILITIES

Best Practice # 10 – Boards exercise fiduciary responsibilities for assets, income, and expenses

---

FIDUCIARY. IT IS a big word that rarely finds its way into our daily conversation. Fiduciary is an adjective meaning, "of or relating to a holding of something in trust for another." That is what boards do, especially related to finances. They hold the mission, plans, staff, systems, funding mechanisms, financial management, and assets in their trust for others. Fiduciary responsibilities are fundamental to the work of the board.

Fiduciary management is …

- **Legal:** Stays in compliance with local, state, and federal laws
- **Smart:** Intelligent care for an organization's assets makes a lot of sense
- **Disciplined:** Ongoing, requiring the diligent application of best practices
- **Practical:** A thoughtful activity that is clear and useful
- **Visionary:** An act of stewardship, faithful today in preparation for tomorrow

At the Murdock Trust, I heard our executive director, Steve Moore, say many times, "Our Trustees steward our mission, our resources, and our leaders." The fiduciary role is one of stewardship, a responsibility never to be taken lightly because of its great potential for good outcomes.

Leadership as Your Most Important Asset

Often I say that when I was a young executive director, the board raised me. The board members did. They cared for me, invested in me, and helped shape my future. Boards must do that, and not just for young leaders and the CEO alone. As organizations grow, the leadership team made up of the CEO and key vice presidents or associates are the number one asset of an organization. I know that in an earlier chapter I emphasized the board's connection to the CEO, but I want to emphasize again that a board's fiduciary and stewardship role must include the CEO and leadership team's professional growth.

Mim Carlson and Margaret Donohoe write, "We have found in our years of nonprofit work that the single most important factor in determining the success of a nonprofit is how well the Executive Director and its Board partner together."[21] This partnership means caring for and investing in your organization's leaders. Additionally, stewardship of the asset of leadership extends to the entire staff. As a result, excellent human resources management practices are always in order, and must be insisted on by the board.

Asset Protection and Risk Management

Besides the leadership and staff, there are many other assets, including program participants and clients, reputation, relationships, information, equipment, cash, investments, and often, the roof over its head. The board must be sure these assets are protected. I recall a church I knew quite well. Its casualty insurance had expired and the board was in the process of deciding about a new carrier. In those few days without coverage the building burned to the ground! The board failed in its fiduciary responsibilities.

Risk Management Tools

Risk management begins with a set of board governing policies, requiring management to implement a board's fiduciary requirements for protecting assets. For example, a policy might read: "The CEO will not fail to see that the organization has comprehensive casualty, liability, and directors and officers insurance to protect the organization from losses and damages." Management's job is to extend board policies, with specific management policies and procedures to reduce risks. To ensure this is being done, a board may conduct a risk management audit every couple of years to satisfy itself that risk management practices are in place. Of course, insurance is essential, as is a way to guard information systems with backup, redundancy, and off-site storage systems. Programs require best practices to reduce risks. The retention of legal counsel and the use of an independent certified public accountant complete the set of risk management tools.

Financial Controls

Your board must insist on a good set of financial controls. Month-end and year-end financial reports are not enough. As a result, most organizations begin with a budget. However, I am of the opinion that a basic set of *board financial policies* should be the beginning point. All subsequent financial practices must align themselves with these board mandates.

Second, these policies require that management expand on them with more *specific policies and procedures* for use by the office, all having been reviewed by a CPA in order to utilize the best practices to build in financial integrity.

Third, an organization needs a *budget*, spread over twelve months so variations of cash flow can be projected. The budget should be realistic, and not a wish book. Yet there also may be an element of stretch to it, especially as an organization is growing. Realism, hard work, and some faith are aspects of budget development and implementation.

Fourth, some type of financial *dashboard* should be created. These are the most important financial measurements worth watching and analyzing in relationship to the past as well as the future. These may relate to specific aspects of your funding model, certain expenses, and bottom line numbers. The utilization of graphs and charts will be helpful in bringing these numbers to life.

More about Financial Policies

Perhaps it is wise for me to comment a little more on the use of financial policies. I've seen boards adopt six pages of financial policies.

I've also seen boards limit their policies to a single page, with management developing the additional policies and procedures. The former may work well for quite small organizations, while the latter is best as nonprofits begin to grow, especially those at the half million mark and more in revenue. One model that offers a snapshot of this practice, and it is only a sample, looks like this:

Purpose: With respect to operating the nonprofit in a sound and prudent fiscal manner, the CEO may not jeopardize the long-term financial strength of the organization. Accordingly, he or she may not:

1. Handle income, donations, expenses, and payroll in a manner that does not provide thorough documentation, safeguards, and checks and balances and use generally acceptable accounting practices
2. Operate without written management policies and procedures that have been reviewed and approved by the organization's CPA
3. Operate without an annual operating budget that has been created by staff and reviewed and ratified by the board
4. Settle payroll and debts other than on time
5. Use or borrow restricted funds from the general operating account for anything other than their intended purpose
6. Allow expenditures to exceed income during the fiscal year except as provided for by a board approved operating budget
7. Allow cash reserves to drop below an amount equal to thirty percent of the annual general operating budget at the midpoint and end of the organization's fiscal year
8. Allow advances from cash reserves for other than ordinary budgeted operating expenses
9. Allow total expenses to deviate by more than five percent above the total operating budget and line item expenses to deviate by more than fifteen percent
10. Operate without receiving a timely, thorough monthly financial report, and not fail to provide the board with timely monthly financial reports
11. Fail to file a board reviewed and approved IRS 990 report or provide year-end financial reports reviewed by a board selected CPA firm,

received by the board's audit committee, and formally approved by the board
12. Fail to communicate with the public each year in an annual report, the essence of the organization's financials

Your organization will likely choose variations of the above policies, but nonetheless, they provide a starting point.

Financial Reporting

Generally an organization's bookkeeper provides monthly reports that include at least a balance sheet and an income and expense report. The latter should include comparisons with the budget. At the end of the year, an independent CPA of the board's choosing should prepare the 990 report (the one that can be found online by the public) for the IRS. As organizations grow, they should also have the CPA prepare annual financials. For small organizations, a basic year-end compilation is in order. As an organization grows, a CPA review is a wise move and should a nonprofit become quite large, or should some funders or agencies require one, an audit will be in order. The board should insist that these reports be prepared and delivered to the board in a timely manner.

Unrestricted Cash

Ah, the magic number, your amount of unrestricted cash. In the great recession, nonprofits that failed to have sufficient sums of available cash found themselves in serious trouble. These are your reserves, unencumbered by restrictions. How much should you have? Enough for one month? Three months? Six months? That is for the board to decide. My point is, you cannot live from hand to mouth, being satisfied that at the end of the month the bills are all paid and there is $1.83 in the bank! Too much time and energy is burned up fussing over finances in an attempt to keep the doors open while neglecting matters that should be of greater importance. Build a reserve for your cash flow needs, emergencies, and unexpected opportunities. Make it a percentage of your budget that is right for your organization.

Your Economic Engine

An organization's mission and programs are supported by what has been called "the enterprise platform" that is made up of organizational capacity (management, support staff, equipment, facilities, and systems) and capital (revenues, unrestricted operating cash and reserves, and fiscal management tools.) Your economic engine is your revenue model, usually made up of contributed and earned income streams, and in some cases, government grants or contracts, and investment earnings. It is essential that diversity be built into each of those streams so an organization does not have to rely on a primary funding source that could rapidly go away. The board must insist that there be a strong economic engine that drives an organization forward.

Boards Don't Raise Money; Board Members Do

Besides insisting that an organization have a sufficient funding model, most people believe boards exist to raise money. I'd like to dispel that myth, and add a few twists.

First, most boards are not made up of high net worth and high profile individuals. Most are made up of people in business, the professions, and community activists. Most are quite ordinary, though the work they do on boards is often quite extraordinary.

Second, boards don't raise money. They govern. Remember the two hats board members wear? As a unit, boards govern when members wear their governance hat.

As individual board members, however, they raise money. Every member puts on his or her volunteer hat. All members help their organization raise money in their own distinct way. Some love to ask others for contributions. Others are great at connecting prospective donors to the organization's staff. Nearly everyone can help thank donors for their contributions. Most are active in some way in helping a nonprofit's fundraising events be a success. But every member is a part of raising money.

Consider the challenge offered by consultant and author Susan Howlett: "Let's invest in our board members so they embrace every aspect of their role with gusto. So they're on fire about the mission and goals, so they understand the context and the budget, so they're clear about what's expected of them and how they can best serve the organization. And let's give them the tools and support they need to connect authentically with donors. Then watch them raise money joyfully."[22]

Finally, board members should be an annual donor of record. The amount is not important, though I do think your donation should be generous. Funders often look for 100 percent participation by the board before they look at the total amount given by the board. So board members set the pace, and CEOs and their development staff can go about the business of raising money knowing their board is committed.

> **Fiduciary:** Holding something in trust for another.
>
> "In resources, the board has three primary areas of interest: people (who are always the heart of the organization), financial enabling, and the physical and soft assets that the people employ ... On the financial side, the finding and dispensing of money undergird the entire operation; each task demands high integrity, and experienced competence."
>
> —Max DePree[23]

Questions for Action

1. Is your board serious about its fiduciary and stewardship role?
2. Does your board make an effort to be sure all assets are protected?
3. Has your board established financial governing policies for management to follow?
4. Does your organization have a diverse funding stream and sufficient unrestricted cash reserves?
5. Are you engaged in helping your organization raise money?

PART 6
SUSTAINING BEST PRACTICES

"Sustainability is an orientation, not a destination."

—Jeanne Bell

Chapter 13

BOARD POLICY MANUAL

Best Practice #11 – Boards govern with a fluid and concise "Board Policy Manual"

BY NOW YOU know I believe that a set of board policies is critical to the governance of an organization. You know I've lived with them, you know I believe they are vital for a nonprofit, and you know I admire the work of John Carver, and have adapted the use of policies in governance. Much of my experience with policies comes from my association with Robert Andringa. So in this section, I will draw heavily on his work which has been the basis for my own experience.

Andringa summarizes the board policy manual (BPM) this way:

> A BPM is the "one voice" of a board of directors that defines for the organization and for itself what on-going policies make the most sense today. It is updated regularly (usually at every meeting) because the world changes. Its contents of 20 or so pages (plus a few attachments) are formulated by both staff and board members, but only the board determines language that stays in the BPM until the next review. Some call it the "governance operating system" that helps a board move from good to great because dozens of good practices get embedded in the BPM.[24]

There are a number of advantages to having a BPM. They help a board avoid a normal pull toward dealing with management issues. They locate all board approved policies in one place. They are available to orient new board members. They clarify authority between the staff and board. And they are the basis for good policy decisions.

What the BPM Is and Is Not

The BPM is not the organization's personnel policy manual, program manual, nor a set of financial policies and procedures. If it were all of these, it could become a rather large set of documents, which could easily become outdated or ignored by the board. Rather, the BPM is the organization's operating system, contained in twenty pages or so of policies. It is a concise document that not only is an active reference point for both management and the board, but it is dynamic and fluid because it is changed with a measure of frequency as changes are needed.

Good Policies

These policies should be:

- **Explicit:** Always in written form
- **Centrally available:** Kept in one document (not years of minutes)
- **Current:** Changed often by the board to reflect current needs
- **Literal:** Meaning what they say, not full of legal jargon
- **Brief:** Not to exceed about twenty or so pages
- **Consistent:** With the law, articles of incorporation, bylaws
- **Comprehensive:** Encompassing the entirety of that which is governed
- **Limited:** Leaving details to management policies written later by the CEO

You may remember the set of board financial policies that appeared in the last chapter. These serve as an example of board policies.

Five Parts to a Good BPM

1. **Introduction and administration:** Defines the reasons for doing a BPM and how it will relate to other board documents, how it is changed, maintained, etc.

2. **Organization essentials:** Includes the mission, vision, values, strategies, major goals, etc., and answers these questions: which benefits? for whom? and at what cost or priority?
3. **Governance structure and process:** Addresses what structure and process the board wants to use, its philosophy of governance, and basic information on meetings, a description of committees, etc.
4. **Board-CEO/staff:** These policies address how the board wants to relate to its one agent, the CEO, and to staff in terms of roles, CEO evaluation, staff benefits, monitoring reports, etc.
5. **Executive parameters:** These executive limitations address what the board does *not* want (or explicitly does want) the CEO and staff to do in pursuing the mission and goals. These generally include funding, financial management, human resources, risk management, and programs. By stating policies in the negative, or as executive limitations, as seen earlier, greater brevity is possible on the board's part and more freedom is given to the CEO for implementation.

Implementing a BPM

All boards can first create a *Board Policy Notebook*, something short of a comprehensive BPM. Here all available existing board approved policies are gathered in one place. Contents may include the bylaws, mission statements, written board roles and responsibilities, financial and human resource policies, conflict of interest policies, and the list goes on. Some will be easy to find while other policies may have to be retrieved from years of board meeting minutes. This document may be all you will create, but at least it is a beginning of moving toward the development of a comprehensive set of board policies in a BPM.

To move forward in developing a BPM, chapter 16 is devoted to a list of resources, so you may want to delve into the work of both Carver and Andringa. The book, *Good Governance for Nonprofits* by Laughlin and Andringa, especially deals with how to develop a BPM.

Implementation begins with a commitment to the concept, and a full buy in by the board and CEO. This includes becoming educated on the subject. Second, the BPM needs to be developed, a task that could be done by a small group over a day or two, or spread out over a period of time. The Laughlin and Andringa book includes a template that will be helpful. Third, the BPM needs to be integrated into the fabric of a board's governing practices. It must become the operating system, used with regularity by both the board and CEO, and updated as needed.

Compliance

It should be stated in the Board-CEO/staff section that the CEO is obligated to inform the board whenever and wherever management is out of compliance with board policies. This allows the board to take any action it deems necessary, but more importantly, creates a high degree of transparency between governance and management functions. When I first began to live under a newly created BPM, the board simply stated, "You have one year to bring everything into compliance." At subsequent meetings the board was informed of our progress in implementing all policies, and at the end of the year, our task was not yet done. So, I informed the board of those policies where I was out of compliance, and which policies were yet to be implemented. An extension was granted and we pressed on.

Board Policy Manual: The singular written voice of a board that defines its policies within one comprehensive living document

"... in our experience, developing a BPM is the most direct way for a nonprofit board to improve the way it governs an organization."
—Fredric Laughlin and Robert Andringa[25]

Questions for Action

1. Are you aware of where to find all board approved policies?
2. Have these policies been assembled in one place?
3. Does it make sense to you to have a basic set of board established policies, and ultimately allow management to create additional operating policies and procedures?
4. Are you interested in further exploration of this strategy for board governance?

Chapter 14

BOARD DEVELOPMENT COMMITTEE

Best Practice #12 – Boards have an active year-round board development committee

MOST EFFECTIVE BOARDS are the result of a high degree of intentionality. For some organizations, building a solid board began on day one. For others, they formed a nonprofit with a founder and a few friends in the room, and the board took on the role of volunteers, cheerleaders, money raisers, and followers of the founder. But over time, the programs grew, and with it, came the necessity of organizational maturity. That meant that the old ways of the board were simply not good enough. The maturing of board governance followed, causing it to make intentional changes.

Where do you and your nonprofit leaders find themselves? Is more maturing needed? Are some of the best practices you've been reading about in need of finding their way into your nonprofit?

Board development is a long-term, ongoing activity. In adopting these twelve best practices, most boards will simply need to make a few major changes, followed by a host of lesser details. These details get down to the specifics, and take considerable time to implement. Many years ago I bought an older Italian sports car, a solid vehicle, but still with a lot of needs. My big decision was to buy and then make repairs, upgrades, and do the necessary restoration work. The details followed, with repeated trips to the garage, and one improvement after another. One day I was looking at the car, and said to myself, "This thing is really looking good!" It didn't happen overnight. It happened as I tended to one detail after another—buffing the paint, replacing trim, fixing upholstery, replacing mirrors, and on and on. Today that Fiat 124 Spider is the queen of my garage. Just as restoring the car required many details carried out over time, building a great board will be the same way. One day it will all come together!

This means that a commitment to build a great board is necessary. That only happens when the CEO, the board chair, and perhaps another key board member begin the process. The full board will eventually follow, though at times there will be resistance to some changes: "We've always done it that way. We've always had a hand in management. We've always met for just an hour. We've had outsiders before who didn't understand and were not as committed as we were. We don't want to make things too complicated." Yet with an intentional commitment, changes will occur over a period of months and years.

Sustaining Best Practices

Not only do those initial changes have to be made, but changes have to be sustained. The BPM is a tool that helps sustain a board because it clearly defines the organization's operating and governing system for all board members. For example, I just reviewed the board recruitment and orientation materials for a Christian high school. And right in the middle of the documents was the BPM. Yes!

The other ingredient is a board development committee that functions year round. I've found that most boards have a person or two who wants to see best practices used, and will commit to see it happen. They should form the nucleus of a board development committee.

It is also important that the CEO have a strong commitment to these best practices, and in some cases, it may be necessary for the CEO to take a lead role in board development.

Organizing the Board Development Committee

Some refer to this group as the governance committee, trustee committee, or even the nominating committee. I like the sound of having a board development committee because it speaks to creating quality, and it opens the door to a number of activities for which some individual or group needs to take responsibility.

The committee must have a chairperson committed to helping build and sustain a great board and another two or three members. In cases of very small boards, the whole board may do the work of the committee in getting board development rolling. It may also be wise to have the board chair involved with the committee. As boards get larger, I find it helpful to have someone on the committee who loves to plan a party.

After all, great boards usually have activities where relationships are built and nurtured.

The committee should meet monthly, and should have a report on its work at every board meeting. Sometimes the committee may come with a proposed new way of doing things that can be discussed, and eventually considered for a vote. Other times the committee will ask the board to look at a list of potential board members and discuss who they think would be the best future candidates.

Eventually the committee should create a handful of annual goals for board development. These should be submitted to the full board for discussion and approval, including a possible budget line item for the board. This will help keep board development activities on track.

Board Development Committee Functions

If a board development committee is to meet year round, just what does it do? Here is a list of possibilities:

- **Bylaws:** Review the bylaws at least annually, and recommend any changes
- **Membership criteria:** Develop, review, and monitor a profile of desired qualifications of new board members
- **New members:** Identify, nurture, screen, orient, and nominate new board members
- **Nominations:** serve as the nominating committee for the election of new members and officers
- **New member orientation:** Conduct a more thorough orientation of new members, including a walk through the BPM
- **Board governance training:** Provide for training in board governance, at a board retreat or short training times at regular meetings (consider using this book with its short chapters as a tool for board development)
- **Nonprofit sector training:** Working with the CEO, provide training that will keep board members up-to-date on trends and practices that are important to your nonprofit's mission
- **Site visits:** Develop and implement a plan whereby every board member personally sees the organization's programs up close

- **Board member evaluation:** Evaluate board members and officers prior to their re-election
- **Board evaluation:** Ongoing evaluation of board size, structure, and processes should be on the table for discussion at least once a year (one board takes five to ten minutes at the end of its meeting, asking the question, "How did we do?")
- **Conflict of interest:** Enforce the conflict of interest policy as it relates to board members
- **Board retreat:** Take the lead in planning an annual board retreat
- **Party:** See that there are social events for board members, their spouses, and special guests (perhaps an annual BBQ, a Christmas season dinner, etc.)

Having a board development committee is a best practice in building and sustaining great board governance.

> **Board Development Committee:** An appointed group of board members charged with sustaining great board governance.
>
> "If you really want to be a successful leader, you must develop other leaders around you. You must establish a team. You must find a way to get your vision seen, implemented, and contributed to by others. The leader sees the big picture, but he needs other leaders to help make his mental picture a reality."
>
> —John Maxwell[26]

Questions for Action

1. Does your board have a governance or board development committee, and if so, what does it do?
2. Who on your board takes the most interest in board development?
3. Which of the committee functions related to building board health are being done by your board?
4. When was the last time your board had any formal governance training?

PART 7
ACQUIRING BEST PRACTICES

"Define actionable things into concrete next steps and successful outcomes."

—David Allen

Chapter 15

TAKING ACTION

U P TO THIS point, I hope the twelve best practices have been informative for you, giving you something to think about, and ultimately act on. I hope you are interested in influencing your board in adopting some of these best practices that may be lacking. I hope you are interested in helping bring great governance to your board. If so, this brief chapter is just for you.

Over the years I've been through a lot of organizational changes. Likely you have too. If you are like me, it is always easier when you are behind the change, rather than having the change done to you. During one of those change processes, I was introduced to William Bridges and his work on change. I especially found his book, *Managing Transitions: Making the Most of Change*, to be helpful. In it he argues that change is situational: a new site, a new boss, new team roles, new policies. These changes are also external to us. Yet some change efforts fall flat. A whole lot of work is done by leaders to change things, but the necessary changes are never fully implemented. This is why Bridges insists that we must do some internal work regarding transitions. He writes, "Situational change hinges on the new thing, but psychological transition depends on letting go of the old reality and the old identity you had before the change took place. Nothing so undermines organizational change as the failure to think through who will have to let go of what when change occurs."[27]

For this to happen, Bridges insists there are three stages of transitions.

First, there is the ending zone, where old practices are let go and put away. You can't do the new while also doing the old. There must be an ending.

Second, there is the neutral zone, the no man's land between the old reality and the new. Here the old way is gone and the new way doesn't yet feel comfortable. Understand that this discomfort is normal. Take your time lest you abort the transition, both personally and organizationally. Without working through this zone, you will jeopardize the changes that are really quite important.

Third, there is the beginning zone. Here the new practices are becoming a reality, and old anxieties that first appeared in the ending zone may be reactivated. After all, doing things a new way represents a gamble. There is risk, but you must move forward with the new practices for them to become effective, and for everyone to become comfortable with them. You will get there, believe me. I've seen it successfully occur.

Seven Steps in Making Changes

The leaders of your board need to follow a series of steps in the adoption of new board best practices. Some will flow smoothly. Others may experience more turbulence.

1. **Identify reasons to make changes with your board:** You must have a motivation
2. **Create a vision for your board:** You must have an emotive big picture of what you want
3. **Determine measurable outcomes:** You must know your destination in tangible, measurable ways
4. **Create action plans:** You must know how you will get there over three-, six-, or twelve-month periods
5. **Identify disciplines:** You must take steps as part of your daily and weekly routine
6. **Be aware of the transition process:** You must keep thinking about your people and how they are moving through the transition process
7. **Identify and celebrate success:** Be aware of and appreciate the successful changes you are making

Once again, change and the adoption of the details of best practices in board governance must be intentional. Follow the steps. Be diligent and be patient. Remember, great board governance will result from the culmination of implementing many new details in how you do things. This will take time. And one day, it will be said of your organization, "They have a great board!"

> "Habit is habit, and not to be flung out of the window by any man, but coaxed downstairs a step at a time."
> —Mark Twain

Chapter 16

RESOURCES

REMEMBER THE THICK books? They have the details, which is why I urge you to avail yourselves of some of the books and resources I've listed in what amounts to an annotated bibliography.

Executive Director Resources

The Executive Director's Guide: Thriving as a Nonprofit Leader by Mim Carlson and Margaret Donahoe (Jossey-Bass). I've recommend this to many nonprofit CEOs, newcomers, and veterans. Their response has been overwhelmingly positive. This is must reading!

The Nonprofit Chief Executive's Ten Basic Responsibilities by Richard Moyers (Board Source). This booklet also belongs on the shelf of the nonprofit CEO.

Board Development

Nonprofit Board Answer Book by Robert Andringa and Ted Engstrom (BoardSource). I've known both of these men and commend their thoughtful answers to your questions.

The Board Governance Series published by Board Source. These nine booklets cover most of the things we've covered but in more detail, and you may well find them quite helpful.

Called to Serve: Creating and Nurturing the Effective Volunteer Board by Max De Pree (Eeerdmans). I like this small book. Businessman and leadership writer Max De Pree utilizes the technique of offering advice to a new CEO about the work of the board. It is classic De Pree, offered with a strong emphasis on the importance of quality personal relationships.

The High-Performance Board: Principles of Nonprofit Organization Governance by Dennis Pointner and James Orilikoff (Jossey-Bass). Here are dozens of details that are part of governing best practices. You will find some gems here. I liked this one a lot.

Governance as Leadership: Reframing the Work of Nonprofit Boards by Richard Chait, William Ryan, and Barbara Taylor (Wiley). Boards are encouraged to go beyond their usual roles of fiduciary and strategic activity into that of generative thinking, engaging with management by wrestling with the larger issues of building organization and mission success. This volume will cause you to think.

Boards on Fire: Inspiring Leaders to Raise Money Joyfully by Susan Howlett (Word & Raby Publishing). The author provides a wealth of experience with boards and fundraising. Her practical insights offered in this short readable volume are of considerable value.

The Five Most Important Questions You Will Ever Ask About Your Organization by Peter F. Drucker and six of his associates (Jossey-Bass). This is a thought-provoking classic that belongs on every leader's bookshelf.

Policy Governance

Boards That Make a Difference, 3rd Ed. By John Carver (Jossey-Bass). I've made a lot of references to John Carver's work, as it has informed my thinking over the years. This is the thick version, in which he fully makes his case for policy governance through ample principles, illustrations, and practical know-how.

The Policy Governance Model and the Role of the Board Member by John and Miriam Carver. I think they knew some would not have the energy to read the large volume, so they wrote this thin booklet. For me, it provides a good refresher, especially since governing with policies takes a measure of discipline.

Good Governance for Nonprofits: Developing Principles and Policies for an Effective Board by Fredric Laughlin and Robert Andringa (American Management Association). I learned how to develop a board policy manual from Bob Andringa before this book was published. I'm glad he and Fredric wrote it. It will be your guide in creating a board policy manual.

There are more books I could suggest to you. But I've already blown your budget if you purchase just a few of these. Nonetheless, I want to suggest that BoardSource has many resources that relate to the details we have been looking at in our twelve best practices. You can find them at www.boardsource.org.

THE AFTERWORD FOREWORD

"If you settle for nothing less than your best, you will be amazed at what you can accomplish in your life."

—Vince Lombardi

OFTEN BOOKS HAVE a foreword, something that needs to be said before the actual book begins. Others have an afterword, something more that needs to be said after the last chapter closes. This is the afterword. But it is really a foreword, because your book on nonprofit governance has not yet been fully written.

Your board likely already exhibits many, if not all of the best practices you have been reading about. Yet I suspect you've had a few "ah-ha" moments, and certainly you've seen where your board comes up short with some of the details. That is not necessarily a criticism. Rather, it is a reality. More can be done in most organizations to help a board move toward great governance.

During the mid-1970s I lived in Portland when the Trailblazers were in their NBA heyday. They won the world championship with Bill Walton as their star player. I was privileged to be in the coliseum for some of the regular season games, and to see how that team performed as a well-oiled machine. The team made Walton great, and Walton made his team members great. They played in harmony, executing well, with a kind of magic.

On the baseball scene in Seattle, I was in the old Kingdome one night when the Mariners were at their best (it is not hard to remember when they were at their best). It was in the Ken Griffey, Jr. years. I watched Junior and three of his teammates hit four homeruns during just five at-bats in a row. Unbelievable!

I tell these stories because like me, you recognize greatness when it is happening. I've also had the privilege to be a part of a few boards and to observe others that exhibited that same kind of magic. Great board members knew what they were doing; they governed well, knew how to make decisions, and how to work in partnership with their CEO. They were passionate about carrying out their nonprofit's mission. Seeing a board function this well, to sense the energy, and to see the results had something in common with a great sports team. Also seeing a board work its way through the muck of hard times, staying loyal, making difficult decisions, and keeping an eye focused on the mission brings the same sense of awe. Great governance, along with an effective CEO, has helped many an organization turn itself around, or has sustained effectiveness over the years.

It's your time now. You have a better grasp of best practices of nonprofit boards. You know some of what needs to be done on your part. You know where to go for more help than this book has to offer. And … you care about the work of your nonprofit. This is your foreword. It's your turn.

ACKNOWLEDGMENTS

IN SOME SENSE, I've been writing this book all of my life, so it is difficult to know where to begin to thank the people who have helped me get to this place. Perhaps I should begin with my first two board chairpersons at Youth for Christ in Tacoma, Stanley Johnson and Paul Stolz. They were businessmen, best friends, and both deeply passionate about their faith and the importance of young people. They also invested deeply in my life, mentoring me, and teaching me the ins and outs of working with a board of directors.

Thanks also go to dozens of other board members for whom I have worked, or with whom I have exercised governance. They all formed the bulwark of the mission of various organizations, and their ability to go about the business of changing lives.

In my years as a Youth for Christ regional executive, I got involved in training and developing boards. The consulting work of Arty Trost first inspired me to train boards. And for more than a dozen years I took the lead in this arena, for both our national and international operations. All of the writing, training, and interactions that were involved helped prepare me to write this book. Thank you, YFC.

A special word of thanks goes to John Carver, whom I have yet to meet. Olan Hendrix first introduced me to policy governance. After having studied under Carver, Olan began going about the country training others. Robert Andringa followed along shortly thereafter, and helped me put into practice what I had been learning about board governance. His writing, friendship, and the opportunity to teach with him, have meant a lot to me.

To my friends at the M. J. Murdock Charitable Trust, thank you. What a ride I had, learning philanthropy at its finest and even better, having the privilege of interacting with passionate and competent nonprofit leaders who in their own space are world changers. If you read this, you know who you are. Thank you.

Finally, a big thanks goes to a fine group of people who took the time to read portions of my writing, offering input, and helping me attempt to get it right. Among them were: Robert Andringa, Janis Bragan Balda, Jay Barber, Joyce Coleman, Chris Ferguson, Fr. Rick Ganz, SJ, Don Goehner, Dennis McMillan, Steven G. W. Moore, Charlie Nipp, Susan Hagen Nipp, Jack Peterson, Todd Silver, Cindy Thompson, William T. Weyerhaeuser, and Walter Wright.

Finally, and most importantly, my thanks go to our family. My wife Joyce, who has loved, encouraged, and supported me, to my three wonderful children, Peter, Anne, and Emily, and to the world's finest grandchildren, I offer my appreciation. All of you have the faith and values I so much admire.

ENDNOTES

Chapter 3: Mission Focused
1. Robert C. Andringa, *Nonprofit Board Answer Book II* (Washington, D.C.: BoardSource, 2002), 15.
2. Peter F. Drucker, *Managing the Nonprofit Organization: Principles and Practices* (New York: HarperCollins, 1990), 45.

Chapter 4 : Quality Membership
3. Charles F. Dambach, *Structures and Practices of Nonprofit Boards* (Washington, D.C: BoardSource, 2003), 18.
4. Max De Pree, *Called to Serve* (Grand Rapids, MI: Eerdmans, 2001), 11.

Chapter 5: Defining Governance
5. John Carver and Miriam Carver, *The Policy Governance Model and the Role of the Board Member* (San Francisco, CA: Jossey-Bass, 2009), 3.
6. Dennis D. Pointner and James E. Orlikoff, *The High Performance Board* (San Francisco, CA: Jossey-Bass, 2002), 2.

Chapter 6: Roles and Responsibilities
7. Max De Pree, p. 53.

Chapter 7: Only the CEO
8. Mim Carlson and Margaret Donohoe, *The Executive Director Guide* (San Francisco, CA: Jossey-Bass, 2010), 78.

Chapter 8: CEO and the Board Chair
9. Robert C. Andringa, from his unpublished *Good Governance Toolbox*
10. Dennis D. Pointner and James E. Orlikoff, 132-133.

Chapter 9: One Voice and Clear Policies
11. John Carver and Miriam Carver, 5.
12. Ibid., 7.
13. Ibid., 7.
14. Ibid., 13.
15. John Carver, *Boards That Make a Difference* (San Francisco, CA: Jossey-Bass, 2006), 191

Chapter 10: Great Board Meetings
16. Richard P. Chait, William P. Ryan, Barbara E. Taylor, *Governance as Leadership* (Hoboken, New Jersey: Wiley, 2005), 6-7, 79
17. Patrick Lencioni, *Death by Meeting* (San Francisco, CA: Jossey-Bass, 2004), viii.

Chapter 11: Accomplishing the Mission
18. John Carver, 90.
19. Drucker, xiv.
20. Peter Drucker, *The Five Most Important Questions* (San Francisco, CA: Jossey-Bass, 2008), xii.

Chapter 12: Fiduciary Responsibilities
21. Mim Carlson and Margaret Donohoe, 139.
22. Susan Howlett, *Boards on Fire* (Seattle, WA: Word & Raby Publishing, 2010)
23. Max De Pree, 32.

Chapter 13: Board Policy Manual
24. Robert Andringa, from his unpublished *Good Governance Toolbox*.
25. Fredric L. Laughlin and Robert C. Andringa, *Good Governance for Nonprofits* (New York: American Management Association, 2007), 24.

Chapter 14: Board Development Committee
26. John C. Maxwell, *Developing the Leaders Around You* (Nashville, TN: Nelson, 1995), 2.

Chapter 15: Taking Action
27. William Bridges, *Managing Transitions* (Cambridge, Massachusetts: Perseus Books, 1991), 2.

ABOUT THE AUTHOR

Dave Coleman is a board governance and management consultant, and principal, for BoardTrek Nonprofit Consulting, a company he founded after over four decades in nonprofit work. During those years he related to boards, and did extensive writing on and teaching governance practices. Most recently he was a grantmaker at the M. J. Murdock Charitable Trust, a foundation in the Pacific Northwest where he became acquainted with hundreds of nonprofits. Prior to that, he worked with youth, served as an executive director, was a regional and national executive, and did extensive board training during his many years with Youth for Christ/USA.

He did his undergraduate work at Whitworth University and holds master's degrees from both George Fox Evangelical Seminary (theological studies) and Chapman University (human resources management). In addition, he studied board governance at Portland State University. He and his wife Joyce reside in Lakewood, a suburb of Tacoma, Washington, where they are active in the life of church and community. They have three adult children as well as grandchildren.

ABOUT BOARDTREK NONPROFIT CONSULTING

BoardTrek Nonprofit Consulting is a small and personal firm whose mission is to serve the common good by guiding organizations on their journey into the future. Specialties include: creating excellence through board governance, strategic planning, leadership development, and organizational change. Our services are custom tailored to meet your needs, using a blend of training, facilitation, writing, and coaching. For more information visit us at www.boardtrekconsulting.com.

> Visit the author at his website to obtain special discount pricing on multiple copies of this book, *Board Essentials*.
>
> www.boardtrekconsulting.com